TENNIS
FOR
ADVANCED PLAYERS

and Those Who Would Like To Be

TENNIS FOR ADVANCED PLAYERS.../

and Those Who Would Like To Be

Jack L. Groppel, PhD

University of Illinois

Human Kinetics Publishers, Inc.
Champaign, Illinois 61820

Production Director: Kathryn Gollin Marshak
Editorial Staff: Margery Brandfon, Sue Wilmoth, and Karen Skrable
Typesetters: Sandra Meier and Carol McCarty
Text and Cover Layout: Lezli Harris
Cover Design: Cary Zimmerman

Cover photograph of Henri LeConte courtesy of AMF Head Racquet Sports

ISBN: 0-931250-57-9
Library of Congress Catalog Number: 83-083164

Printed in the United States of America.

10 9 8 7 6 5 4 3 2 1

Human Kinetics Publishers, Inc.
Box 5076   Champaign, IL 61820

To my parents,
Howard and Pauline Groppel.
Thanks for everything.

Jack

Contents

Chapter 3   **FOOTWORK'S THE NAME OF THE GAME**   **35**

Chapter 4   **CONTROL VERSUS POWER**   **53**

Preface

Competitive tennis players are usually willing to try anything to gain a slight edge over an opponent. That's why tennis players and coaches all over the world are continually searching for ways of improving performance. Often these individuals receive their information from a relatively new area of expertise called *sport science*. Many subdisciplines exist under the major heading of sport science: sport biomechanics, exercise physiology, and sport psychology are a few. Each has its own relative importance to the tennis player, whether it's a new method of physical conditioning, a unique approach to psychological training, or an improved performance technique. Technique improvement in tennis falls in the area of biomechanics, which will be the portion of sport science covered by this book.

Biomechanics is the study of human motion. A tennis biomechanist analyzes a player's efficiency of movement and tries to determine whether a player could perform more effectively. The biomechanist will also be on the lookout for stressful movements that may create trauma to certain body parts. In addition, biomechanics is concerned with designing equipment that is most suitable to you and your tennis game. It is the information gained from biomechanical principles and their practical application to tennis that will make this book helpful in answering the numerous questions of the advanced player and coach.

When skilled tennis players are working on their games, they often search for one specific result: perfect form. They try to achieve perfection in many ways, but the most popular — and often the most hazardous — is modeling a specific pro player. This brings up a significant question; one, in fact, that could serve as the general theme for this book. Is there a perfect way to play tennis?

What professional tennis player has the best form? Is it McEnroe, Evert Lloyd, Connors, or Navratilova? Your guess is as good as mine. I don't think there really is an absolutely perfect way to play tennis. All of the pros I've mentioned swing the racquet with specific idiosyncracies. In fact, depending on what grip a player uses, there are many different ways to swing a tennis racquet and still hit the ball effectively. That's why a player shouldn't try to mimic the technique of one certain player. You never know if there are specific reasons for playing the way he or she does. For instance, McEnroe's service stance has been ridiculed a great deal, but many players (especially the younger ones) nevertheless idolize John and want to play like him. They don't realize that he began using that service stance as a youth due to a strained back. He would stretch the muscles in his back in this position and it made him feel more comfortable. Therefore, John started using that service stance for medicinal reasons — not to make his serve stronger. It's for reasons such as this that players should base their techniques on what is best for them and not on what specific pros do when they hit a certain stroke. Thus, we can honestly say that no professional tennis player has perfect form in all situations.

Actually, there is only one point during the swing when perfection must occur: when the ball is on the racquet face. It doesn't matter what your stroke looks like as long as the ball is hit correctly. When Borg first entered the tennis scene his forehand was said to be so unorthodox that he would never make it big and, even if he had a shot at being a great player, his career would be cut short by tennis elbow. Borg's career aside, there is one thing that can be said about his forehand: At impact he was nearly perfect in hitting the ball how he wanted to and where he wanted to. This is definitely one factor that separates great players from good players. The good tennis players don't hit the ball as effectively as they could.

The application of sport science concepts can offer much information on how tennis players can improve their strokes. I've already said that there may not be a perfect way to play tennis, but the use of sport science principles will enable you to optimize your current techniques. It will not necessarily change them completely but it will manicure them into a better product for competition. The purpose of this book is to meet that end. In the first few chapters you will be exposed to sport science concepts and how they apply to various aspects of tennis, to the development and design of the varied equipment used in tennis, and to footwork. The subsequent chapters deal with advanced stroke development, including such topics as how to generate more force yet maintain control and how to effectively use spin.

This book will not offer you a cookbook orientation to tennis. Instead, it will provide you with proven, researched information about improving your tennis game. The laws of science govern all types of human motion and the application of these laws has been heavily utilized by Olympic athletes intent on breaking world records. There is no reason to prevent this from carrying over to tennis. In fact, there exists an incredible amount of sport science data that can be used by the tennis-playing public. The problem in the past has been in bridging the gap between the sport scientist and the athlete. I hope that this dilemma has been resolved because it seems that today's players are ready for such an approach to tennis. In actuality, the modern tennis player has specific needs that must be answered. This book deals with some of those needs in an applied manner which all tennis enthusiasts and students of the game will hopefully understand and enjoy.

Jack L. Groppel, Ph.D.

ACKNOWLEDGMENTS

Many people have had a major role in the development of my career. To all of them I owe a great deal of gratitude. But mere thanks isn't enough for those who have had a significant impact on teaching me to apply biomechanics and research to the game of tennis. In addition, credit should be given to those who assisted me in putting this book together.

Special thanks should go to the individuals who were heavily involved in my education: Chuck Dillman, Bob Singer, and Terry Ward.

I would also like to extend my gratitude to those whose lives are already dedicated to tennis and whom I have worked with along the way: Tim and Tom Gullikson, Stan Smith, Jim Loehr, Robert Nirschl, and Vic Braden.

A special acknowledgment should go to the following persons, whose technical expertise helped to make this book possible: Barb Young, Margie Brandfon, Terri Bodecker, Bill Aull, Peter Bouton, and Pamela Wilson. Special thanks should go to my good friend, Chuck Mercer, whose skill in photography was particularly valuable to the completion of this book.

Finally, I want to offer my sincere appreciation to those who have given me understanding and encouragement even during the roughest of times: Sue Arildsen, Bill Wicks, Ruth Ann Kincaid, and my parents.

TENNIS
FOR
ADVANCED PLAYERS

and Those Who Would Like To Be

Bridging the Gap: The Quest for a Perfect Game

GLOSSARY

Acceleration — Rate of change of velocity.

Angular Momentum — The angular force generated by a body based on its resistance to rotation multiplied by its velocity of rotation.

Ground-Reaction Force — The force emitted from the ground as a body pushes against it.

Linear Momentum — The linear force generated by a body based on its mass multiplied by its velocity.

Sport Science — The application of scientific principles to movement activities in sport.

Torque — An angular force that occurs about a joint.

What does it take to win Wimbledon? First, you must be in excellent physical condition. Then you must be ready to compete under extreme psychological pressure. But before these ever come into play, you've got to have the strokes. They don't need to be aesthetically pleasing, but they must be effective. In addition, the more efficient your strokes are the less energy you'll need to expend. When your tennis strokes are both effective and efficient, the results can be devastating to your opponent. However, it's another matter when your game lacks one of these elements. If your shots lack effectiveness you may lose the match, but even worse, if they lack efficiency, you may be injured. This is where sport science can help your game; it can make you both effective and efficient. Take the case of Stan Smith, for example.

Classic and picture perfect are only some of the terms that were used to describe Stan Smith's service motion. His serve was so effective, in fact, that it led the way for Stan's number 1 world ranking in the early 1970s. His domination of tennis diminished in the mid-1970s, however, partially due to severe elbow pain. The pain became so severe that Smith needed surgery.

Prior to the operation, Smith decided to determine what had caused his problem: whether it was simply stress from overuse or whether it stemmed from a flaw in stroke production. To find out, Smith had high-speed movies taken of himself during a workout. The films, played back at normal speed, revealed no apparent error in stroke mechanics. But when the films were viewed in stop-action the problem with his serve became clear. When Smith reached a point in his service motion near the *backscratch* position his hand turned under and the racquet head deviated to the side of his body (Figure 1-1). This extraneous movement placed an incredible amount of force on the inner part of his elbow. Scar

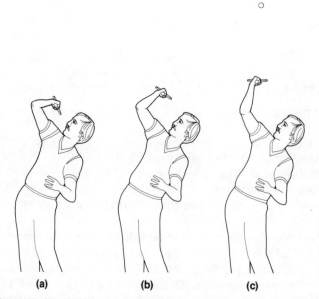

(a)   (b)   (c)

Figure 1-1(a), (b), (c) In these diagrams (drawn from consecutive movie frames taken at 100 frames per second), you can see the problem Stan Smith had with the positioning of his racquet, hand, wrist and elbow.

(a)   (b)

Figure 1–2(a), (b),   Stan Smith changed his full windmill type serving
action to the half-swing method seen in these pictures.

tissue built up as the body's defense mechanisms tried to protect the
joint. Unfortunately, this protective scarring caused Smith considerable
pain so the scar tissue had to be removed and the elbow surgically
repaired.

Following the operation, Smith wanted to change his serve to prevent any recurrence of elbow trauma. Although no change could offer
100% assurance, a serving method was suggested to lower the possibility
of injury. Instead of using a full windmill action that allowed his hand to
turn under during the backscratch part of the loop, Smith employed a
half-swing method in taking the racquet back (Figure 1-2). This new motion still allowed him an adequate amount of body rotation yet prevented
too much hand movement at the top of his swing. In addition, when he
got to the top of his swing Smith was told to keep the palm of his hand
toward his head, further preventing it from turning under. Smith practiced this new motion until it became natural and tried it immediately
upon his return to the circuit: He won the Australian Tournament of
Champions in one of his first competitive events.

Here is a world-class athlete whose service motion was considered
by many to be the perfect form. The one small flaw in Stan Smith's serve,

and the one that caused him so much pain, was never picked up by the naked eye. Instead, it took a specific view from a high-speed film analysis to determine the problem.

Stan Smith's problem was one of stroke efficiency; but sport science cannot only help tennis players become more efficient, it can also help them become more effective. For example, I recently had the opportunity to work with a former runner-up in the Florida State Closed Clay Court Championship. This tennis player had a very good weapon in his forehand, but he only used his two-handed backhand to keep the ball in play. It wasn't a very penetrating shot, so he asked me to take a look at his stroke and let him know what I thought. After rallying for about 10 or 15 minutes his problem became apparent. He did not understand how to use body rotation in hitting a two-handed backhand, so his technique involved very little hip and trunk rotation and a great deal of arm action (see Figure 1-3). By separating the movements of his trunk and upper limbs during the forward swing he had very little force behind the stroke. What I told him to do was to step toward the ball as he had been doing. However, I wanted him to rotate his hips and trunk and let his arms swing forward with his trunk rather than swinging so much like a baseball player. Being a skilled tennis player, it only took him about 15 minutes to understand how the hips and trunk should work together in bringing the arms and racquet toward impact (see Figure 1-4). He was amazed at how hard he actually was able to hit the ball after only another

(a)   (b)   (c)

Figure 1-3(a), (b), (c) This is an ineffective two-handed backhand. Note how little hip rotation occurs, which makes the trunk and upper limbs work harder.

(a)   (b)   (c)

Figure 1-4(a), (b), (c)   This is an efficient two-handed backhand which sufficiently employs the hips and trunk to transfer force to the upper limb.

30 minutes of practice. Since one of his goals is to play on the professional tour, he needed a mechanical analysis to bring together his body parts in hitting an effective two-handed backhand. Thus, in this example sport science increased a player's effectiveness by improving his technique.

Sport science can also help the tennis enthusiast with equipment design. For example, in the mid-1970s, Howard Head invented the oversized racquet and presented it to contemporary tennis society. Head, who turned the entire skiing industry around with the production of metal skis, had the audacity to suggest that tennis players might be able to hit the ball more effectively with this new racquet. Although Head's oversized racquet soon became the brunt of many tennis jokes, the ridicule lasted only as long as it took people to realize that what he was saying was true. His racquet was found to have a larger hitting zone and to decrease the vibrations and oscillations transmitted to the hand from impact. Head's new racquet seemed to give a psychological advantage as well; beginners and advanced players began to feel secure when using the larger head because they felt that they simply couldn't miss!

HOW CAN SPORT SCIENCE HELP YOUR GAME?

Although we've seen how specific applications of sport science have helped some athletes, the next step becomes applying this knowledge to

Figure 1-5 Here, you can see one of Jimmy Connors' patented "jumping" forehand drives.

you. One question you need to ask yourself is "what must I do to make my strokes more effective and efficient?" Some very basic physical laws apply to tennis that could help you become a better player.

One of the most important and most common of these principles is Newton's Third Law: For every action there is an equal and opposite reaction. A good example of this is ground-reaction force. It's a fact that much of the force a player generates when hitting a shot comes from the ground. Any tennis player who tries to pulverize every shot by jumping into it is only looking for trouble. Although Jimmy Connors (Figure 1-5) often jumps when hitting his patented high-velocity ground strokes, Figure 1-6 shows that he doesn't leave the ground until the instant of impact. Therefore, he does generate a high ground-reaction force and the jumping doesn't contribute greatly to his strokes. Connors' main sources of force come from two other physical principles: linear and angular momentum.

Linear momentum is simply transferring body weight forward. Your tennis teacher probably told you to step into the ball on every shot (see Figure 1-7). In actuality, the coach was telling you to generate linear momentum into the stroke. Once you've transferred your linear momentum forward, angular momentum should come into play. Angular

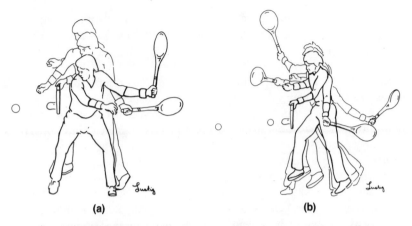

(a)   (b)

Figure 1-6(a), (b) As Jimmy Connors hits a forehand drive, notice that he doesn't leave the ground until his stroke is very near the point of impact.

momentum is produced from body rotation occurring at the hips and trunk. There are very few shots in tennis where the athlete can be effective without using angular momentum. To realize its importance, try hitting a forehand drive without rotating your trunk; it won't be one of your better shots.

Stability also plays a large role in tennis. Anyone wishing to excel must strive to be in a balanced state whenever possible. This doesn't mean that you must be perfectly still each time you hit a ball nor does it

Figure 1-7 This player demonstrates how to transfer linear momentum forward into a forehand drive.

mean that you shouldn't hit a ball on the run. It simply means that your body must be in control when swinging the racquet toward impact. By lifting the shoulders too early in a stroke or by continually hitting off the back foot you only increase the likelihood of making an error. Even when you hit a shot while running at full tilt, your upper body must be under control to bring the racquet forward properly.

Once you understand these concepts, you need only one more before preparing to upgrade your mastery of the game. That concept is Newton's Second Law: Force = Mass × Acceleration. As you have no control over your mass it is always a constant. Therefore, force is directly proportional to acceleration. In other words, the greater the acceleration, the more force you'll provide. The player in Figure 1-8 has accelerated his racquet head to almost the maximum. But remember, tennis isn't really a game of high-velocity shots as much as it's a game of control.

A good velocity/accuracy trade-off involves hitting a shot with a certain amount of speed, yet not so fast as to impede accuracy. Your stroke must depend on the velocity of your opponent's oncoming shot, where he or she is located on the court, and how you have to return the ball. If your opponent is at the net, for example, you wouldn't want to hit a soft floater that clears the net by 5 or 6 feet. The shot you select to hit (whether it's a drive, lob, or even an angled dink shot) must be hit with the proper velocity to maintain maximum control. This requires good tennis stroke mechanics.

Obviously, there is more to the mechanics of tennis than Newton's Laws of Motion. However, this preliminary information will serve as a

Figure 1-8 This player is swinging the racquet as hard as he possibly can. Although he is accelerating to provide a great amount of force to the ball, his control is likely to be poor.

good foundation for the subsequent chapters dealing with stroke production. By having a thorough understanding of these physical laws, applying them to your strokes, and analyzing the strokes of highly skilled tennis players your game could improve significantly.

WHAT CAN YOU LEARN FROM WATCHING A PRO?

Before discussing how you can benefit from critiquing a professional tennis player's game, you need to distinguish the difference between an important performance characteristic and a mere idiosyncracy. Let's examine a couple of the more well-known idiosyncracies on the pro tour.

Chris Evert Lloyd has a great following among all levels of tennis enthusiasts. This following is so large that many players want to play just like Chris. She would be an excellent model to identify with if the right things were copied. For example, when Chris hits a forehand she holds her left arm out to the side and positions her hand so it's open and almost perpendicular to her forearm (Figure 1-9a). There's nothing wrong with doing this, but you should be aware that it has nothing to do with her great forehand. Instead of copying the left-hand motion of her forehand, players should watch how the left arm moves in relation to the right arm (see Figure 1-9b). Then you'll see how she uses trunk rotation (angular momentum) to hit an effective forehand drive.

(a)　　　　　　　　　　　　　　　　(b)

Figure 1-9(a), (b)　Observe Chris Evert Lloyd's left-hand position as she hits a forehand drive. Note in picture b how her left arm moves in synchrony with the right arm, which demonstrates the amount of trunk rotation she uses.

(a)   (b)

Figure 1-10(a), (b) Picture a depicts John McEnroe's starting position for his serve. Although his service stance has been criticized, you will learn from the subsequent chapters how he utilizes this starting position to maximize his body rotation (b).

John McEnroe's stroke mechanics provide another example of playing idiosyncracies, although his are a bit more difficult to see than Evert Lloyd's. Many tennis authorities believe McEnroe's stroke mechanics are actually very poor, and if it weren't for his outstanding athletic ability he would struggle in professional tennis. One reason for this public opinion is McEnroe's awkward serving stance (Figure 1-10). It's true that few teaching pros would ever recommend this starting position. However, close examination of McEnroe's serve reveals that he actually generates a great deal of body rotation during the motion. Therefore, his starting position isn't as bad as it might seem. It's his mechanics of motion prior to impact that make him a great server.

When watching a highly skilled player don't be so attentive to extraneous motions, but concentrate on how the player actually moves to swing the racquet. Make note of various body movements and how the player generates force to hit a ball. Pick out certain body parts and watch only these areas during a specific stroke, attempting to determine how each segment contributes to the final outcome. This approach could literally open your eyes to many aspects of how to play the best tennis you possibly can.

As you continue the quest to improve your game, strive for a good velocity/accuracy trade-off. This will increase the effectiveness of your strokes. In addition, remember that tennis is not played with the upper limb alone. Force should be generated from the ground and transferred through your body to the swinging limb through a combination of linear and angular momentum. This sequencing of forces between body parts will not only enable you to hit more penetrating shots, but it also will improve your efficiency in playing the game.

CHAPTER **2**

Optimize
Your Game
with the Proper
Equipment

GLOSSARY

Foot Pronation — When the sole of the foot turns outward.

Friction — The opposing force between two contacting surfaces (e.g., a shoe sole and a court surface).

Heel Counter — A stabilizing and supporting device that controls rear foot motion and helps to hold your foot in the shoe.

Heel Cup — The area in the rear of a tennis shoe that holds the heel of your foot.

Hitting Zone — The area on a racquet face where the most effective impact will occur.

Moment of Inertia — A body's resistance to rotation.

Nap — The synthetic wool covering on a tennis ball.

Oversized Racquet — Any midsized or jumbo tennis racquet.

Racquet Face — The area on a racquet where the strings are located.

Racquet Head — The frame portion of the racquet that contains the strings.

Shoe Last — The form that the shoe is shaped around.

Toe Box — The area toward the front of a tennis shoe that contains the forward portion of your foot.

Torque — An angular force that causes rotation.

It doesn't matter what tennis equipment we use! It's all engineered way beyond any of our physical capabilities! This phrase has been seen in print or heard in lectures quite often over the past few years. It is actually correct if you are speaking purely of how various pieces of equipment perform in laboratory tests. But isn't there more to the selection of tennis equipment than mere laboratory performance? What about such things as how a racquet feels when you hit an aggressive volley, how well your new shoes allow you to slide into a shot on clay, or how that new can of tennis balls holds up after two sets on hard courts? These factors and many more are important determinants in selecting tennis equipment. Perhaps that's why F.W. Danisthorpe in his 1933 writings on the *Mechanics of Lawn Tennis* spent five pages describing stroke production and strategy while devoting nine pages to the design and function of tennis balls and racquets. He continually cited what a problem it was for the player to decide what equipment to use.

The problems of selecting tennis equipment for the tennis player in 1933 were nothing compared to those of today's player (Figure 2-1). The 1933 player had only one racquet composition available: wood. Today

Figure 2-1 This is probably how most of us feel when trying to select a tennis racquet.

we have wood, metal, fiberglass, graphite, boron, and various composites of these materials. Selecting a tennis shoe or a type of ball wasn't nearly as complicated either simply because there weren't as many to choose from.

There are numerous reasons given to explain why tennis equipment has proliferated. First, engineering technology has advanced to enable manufacturers to discover and synthesize new materials. Not only have the types of materials changed, but so have the designs of the equipment. Tennis shoes, for example, used to be made only with rubber soles and only on one style of shoe last. Rubber can still be found in shoe soles; but several shoe lasts are currently available which fit different types of feet and conform to different types of foot motion. There really seems to be no end in sight for the sophistication of tennis equipment. The only end may be caused by the pocketbook of the many tennis players who won't spend $300 for a racquet frame.

The tennis boom of the late 60s and early 70s is a second reason for so many types of tennis paraphernalia. With millions of individuals taking up the game the manufacturing business became very lucrative. Greater varieties of equipment were produced as product designers attempted to keep up with demand and maintain an edge over competitors.

Not only is tennis being played by millions of people, it is played in all kinds of environments: humid coastal areas, mountain resorts, beautiful indoor clubs, gymnasiums, and so on. Depending on where the game is played, different equipment is needed. For example, the mountain resorts need high-altitude tennis balls, and the humid coastal areas need synthetic strings because gut may not last as long.

It seems that manufacturers are meeting the demand. More equipment is being designed and developed that answers the needs of all tennis players. However, little is ever said about what equipment type is best suited for what individual. For example, a player walks into a store to buy a racquet. There are racquets of all compositions, sizes, and shapes on the shelf. There are usually no strings in the racquet, so the player has to choose a string type and tension. Each racquet has a specific grip size and weight. These factors all play a role in how a racquet will perform for a certain player. Therefore, we need to examine each factor and determine its importance for the advanced tennis player.

RACQUET MATERIALS AND FLEXIBILITY

Many of today's manufacturers have stated that wooden racquets are outdated and don't offer the performance of newer materials. This may be true in the laboratory, but I wonder if wood is really that bad, especially when you consider that some great players — Evert Lloyd, Curren, Austin, and Mandlikova, — still use wood. Granted the trend is toward the graphite composites because of their high performance, but don't sell wood short. It can still offer good results.

Out of all the materials available, graphite is known to dampen the vibrations of impact more than any other. This is good news for the player afflicted with tennis elbow. Few racquets, however, are made solely of graphite. Graphite usually is combined with fiberglass or some other high-performance material. This often forms a stiff racquet that behaves extremely well on a short, aggressive stroke like a volley.

Manufacturers usually classify their racquets as stiff, medium flexibility, and flexible — although these classifications are not consistent among manufacturers. A racquet categorized as stiff by one manufacturer might be placed in the medium-flexibility class by another. However, don't be concerned with these inconsistencies. You should be aware of this: Research has shown that a racquet classified near the stiff end of the continuum will yield a higher ball velocity than a racquet categorized toward the flexible end of the continuum (Brody, 1979). With a flexible racquet, energy is lost as the shaft bends in reaction to impact. A stiff racquet will not deform as much and the ball will not lose as much energy.

What is it that causes one racquet to be stiffer than another? Surprisingly enough, it's not the materials used to make the racquet as much as it is the racquet's shape. As a rule, the smoother the transition from the widest part of the racquet head to the handle, the more likely it is to be stiff. Materials used to make the racquet do play a role, however.

When purchasing a racquet be aware of how it's put together. If it seems that different pieces of wood have been laminated together, as in Figure 2-2, the stiffness of the racquet won't vary much from others

Figure 2-2 In this photo you can see how various laminations of wood are pieced together to make a racquet.

made in a similar fashion. However, if the manufacturer has added fiberglass or graphite into the frame, the racquet's stiffness may become more dependent on this reinforcement. The more graphite found in a racquet, the stiffer the racquet will be. As for aluminum racquets, stiffness is again more dependent on design than on materials. One piece of aluminum is as strong, within 2%, as another piece of aluminum. Some aluminum alloys are stronger than others, but they are not necessarily stiffer in relation to how they would react to impact by a tennis ball. The shape and cross section of the metal actually determines the racquet's stiffness. As a rule, the bulkier the tubing or metal extrusion, the stiffer the racquet.

Before you decide what racquet flexibility you should have, analyze your own game style. If you like to rush and crush (serve and volley), a stiffer racquet may be what you need. Remember that volleys are very short strokes and you need a quick response from the racquet. However, if a baseline game better describes your playing style, you may want to try a more flexible shaft. Ball velocity shouldn't be as high on your priority list as ball control.

Now that you've got an idea of what racquet flexibility might best fit your game, you have to consider the size of the racquet head with which you wish to play. Some of you may already know, but for those who don't I'll discuss what sport science tells us about the various designs.

Racquet Head Design—The Shape of the Future

During the 1981 Avon Championships of Oakland, Andrea Jaeger was playing Pam Shriver in a nationally televised match. At one point in the match, Jaeger lobbed to the 5'11" Shriver, only to have Shriver drill an overhead smash. The commentator, Mary Carillo (a former world-class player herself), immediately said, "Wow! Shriver is tall but she's even taller with that oversized racquet." Obviously, Pam wasn't any taller, but with an oversized racquet in her hand she became an ominous figure at the net. Thus, one effect of the oversized racquet is opponent intimidation (Figure 2-3). Another significant effect of the jumbo racquets is the psychological confidence they give some players. This is so prevalent, in fact, that I call it the *I Can't Miss* syndrome.

When the first oversized racquet hit the market a few years ago, most people saw it as another fad. It was called a snowshoe, a screen door, a rug beater, and so on. But we all made a big mistake by not buying stock in the oversized-racquet industry. Today a high percentage of professional and college players use an oversized racquet. I will even go out on a limb to say that in about ten years you will walk onto public courts and find that the conventional racquet will be midsized or oversized, while today's conventional racquet will be the odd-looking one.

Figure 2-3 Imagine what this player could do with a return if he got his racquet on it (photograph by Arthur Shay).

Well, what's so special about an oversized racquet? Does it play better? Does it absorb shock more effectively? Or is it just a psychological placebo, a fad, which has little effect on playing ability?

Prior to the tennis boom, a tennis player didn't have to worry about frame size when selecting a racquet. There was only one racquet head shape: an ellipse. It's performance was never questioned — until the manufacturers began their heavy-duty competition to get ahead in sales. The search for a better racquet began. New materials were examined, but not nearly to the extent as was the structure of the racquet head. As a result, the elliptical racquet head is virtually outdated and is being replaced by teardrop, square, round, and oval shapes. The important outcome of these new designs is the larger racquet face usually provided by each. But how will that larger face affect performance for advanced players? Research in this area has just begun, but some of the findings are relevant to you.

The Application of Sport Science to Racquet Head Design

The majority of tennis racquet research has studied the difference in the increased racquet face size found in most of the new designs relative to the size of the traditional, elliptical racquet head. Whether a

Moment of Inertia = A racquet's resistance to rotation = mass (m) x radius (r)^2

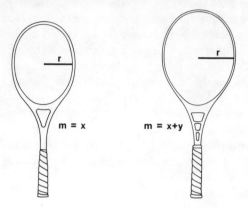

Figure 2-4   This diagram shows how the moment of inertia of a racquet head can be increased to reduce rotation during and following impact.

racquet head is conventional sized, midsized, or oversized, two concepts will hold true: When a ball hits in the center of the racquet face, the net force to the hand following impact will be negligible. However, when a ball hits off-center on the racquet face (which most do regardless of racquet head size) the racquet tends to twist along its long axis. This twisting effect, or torque, could have severe effects on the shot and cause serious strain to your forearm muscles as they contract to control excessive racquet movement.

Brody (1979) suggested that this twisting may be reduced by increasing the moment of inertia of the racquet head. The moment of inertia (I) of an object is a measure of that object's resistance to rotation (Figure 2-4). Its magnitude is dictated by a simple equation, $I = mr^2$, where m is the object's mass and r is its radius. Therefore, two ways exist to increase the moment of inertia of a racquet head so that the twisting effect will be reduced: (1) by increasing the size of the racquet head and (2) by adding small weights to the perimeter of the racquet head. Both methods have been used, but the most popular is to increase the racquet head size. Howard Head found that by making a racquet 20% wider, the twisting potential was reduced by almost 40%. As for the sports medicine implications of this phenomenon, Dr. Robert Nirschl, an orthopedic surgeon, has collected extensive data on patients afflicted when using an oversized racquet (personal communication). His data actually favored the midsized racquet head over the jumbo.

Besides reducing the twisting effect, widening the racquet head and/or adding perimeter weights has another effect on the racquet. It increases the effective hitting zone of the racquet face by as much as four times. In addition, Dr. Bruce Elliott (1980) has shown that oversized racquets are better able to absorb the vibrations produced by off-center impacts both toward the sides and ends of the racquet face. On the court playing tests by Blanksby, Ellis, and Elliott (1979) have also shown that the oversized racquet is ". . . equal to, or superior to, conventional racquets where stroke accuracy of recreational players is concerned. . . ."

Even with all this supporting information favoring the oversized racquet, it still comes under fire when discussed among advanced players. They are usually concerned with ball velocity and the racquet's overall performance. However, it's a fact that the majority of world-class men and women players use a midsized or jumbo racquet. In addition, Dr. Elliott found that when comparing impact rebound velocities between conventional racquets and their oversized counterparts, the latter produced significantly higher velocities.

Selecting a Racquet Based on Your Needs

Skilled tennis players should be extremely aware of their equipment's performance relative to their personal needs and game style. If you are basically a baseline player, you may want to avoid an extremely stiff racquet and use a medium-flexible or flexible racquet. In contrast, if you play an aggressive serve-and-volley game, you may want the rigid performance offered by a stiffer racquet. You should be aware that the trend of consumer usage is toward the midsized and jumbo racquets. Laboratory studies and play tests have shown the beneficial effects of these racquets over the conventional, smaller racquet head. With the increased hitting zone in these oversized racquets it also makes sense that accuracy will be improved. Finally, for those afflicted with any type of arm pain while they play, sport science has shown that graphite reduces the shock of impact more than other materials; the same has been found for the oversized racquet.

Once you've decided what racquet type and flexibility will be most appropriate, the final decision on your hand-held equipment still cannot be made. You must consider what string type and tension you need to best fit your needs.

STRING TYPES AND TENSIONS

For years, average recreational tennis players were told at the time of a racquet purchase to string their racquet with nylon at 55 pounds tension. It was thought that this string type and tension would produce optimum playability regardless of game style and give the racquet a healthy life span. The advanced player was told to string his or her racquet looser for more control and tighter for more velocity. This thinking has recently caused quite a bit of controversy. Today's tennis player has a hard time

believing such advice because they have read that Borg strung his racquets at 80 pounds when he was most successful and that McEnroe
strung his conventional racquet at around 48 pounds. How can you be
told to string your racquets at a specific tension when two of the best
players in the world string their racquets so differently? World-class
athletes obviously string their racquets according to their personal needs.
So why shouldn't you? Let's begin by discussing what sport science has
shown us about string types.

Gut Versus Nylon

The most commonly misunderstood type of string is gut. Gut is
manufactured from the smooth-muscle portion of sheep or beef in-
testine; it is elastic and resilient because it contains a low percentage of
fat. Gut, once extracted from the animal, undergoes a thorough chemical
process of washing, bleaching, twisting, drying, and refining to insure
strength and uniformity. Some gut string is then waterproofed to give it a
longer life (especially in high humidity).

Other types of string include nylon, artificial gut, graphite string,
oil-filled string, and so on. Most of these are synthetic but this prolifera-
tion of string varieties only adds to the significant problem encountered
by most players. How is one to select a string type?

It all depends on what you want from the string. Little is actually
known about the many types of synthetic string, but if cost is of greatest
importance, nylon is inexpensive, durable, and long lasting. Many string
manufacturers claim that their synthetic products play like gut. Although
it's possible, it's not probable. It is extremely difficult to produce a string
that behaves like natural gut. Player evaluations have shown gut to provide better control, higher resultant ball velocities, lower vibration levels
to the hand, and improved overall playability. In addition, Ellis, Elliott,
and Blanksby (1978) demonstrated that tests on resultant ball velocity of
gut and synthetic gut strung at the same tension favored the gut string.
But how do different string types behave at different tensions?

String Tension

Bruce Elliott continued his experiments with varying string tensions to
include an analysis of gut versus nylon and their effects on ball velocity.
He found that, regardless of whether gut or nylon were used, ball
velocity decreased when string tension went from 50 pounds to 65
pounds. However, when comparing gut string to nylon at the same levels
of tension, he concluded that ball velocities following impact were
"superior in favor of gut string."

The effect of varying string tensions should be important to skilled
players who wish to optimize their play. The tension used by a player can

**TABLE 2-1   The Effects of String Tension
on Postimpact Ball Velocity (from Groppel, 1983)**

String Tension (lb)	Average Ratio* of Postimpact Ball Velocity / Preimpact Ball Velocity
40 (n = 10)[a]	.503
50 (n = 10)	.482
60 (n = 10)	.467
70 (n = 10)	.463

*The higher this ratio, the higher the rebound velocity relative to the ball velocity before impact.
[a]n = 10 refers to the 10 trials that were measured at each tension.

have a tremendous effect on shot velocity and control. My colleagues and I recently conducted an experiment to examine these effects. As balls were fired against a fixed racquet, films taken at 500 frames per second were used to determine the ratio of postimpact ball velocity to preimpact ball velocity. This was done for the same racquet strung with nylon at four different tensions (40 lb, 50 lb, 60 lb, and 70 lb).

From Table 2-1, you can see that a progression of ratios exist from 40 to 70 lb with 40 lb producing the highest ball velocities. This puts a new perspective on the advice for string tension and ball velocity: The looser the strings (within reason), the higher the postimpact ball velocity. One explanation might be that the lower the string tension, the more the strings will deflect on impact and the less energy will be absorbed from the ball, which will cause the ball to leave with a faster rebound velocity. That is, the ball will deform less and lose less energy. Subsequently, the ball will rebound with more energy and will have a higher velocity. Another explanation might be that the larger the portion of energy maintained in the strings, the greater the effect on ball rebound velocity provided the time of ball contact with the strings matches the time of string deflection and repositioning (Brody, 1979). A trampoline effect may then occur as some of the energy stored in the strings during impact is returned to the ball, thus increasing the rebound velocity.

Velocity must be used with optimal control to play highly skilled tennis. To study the effects of string tension on control, I took films at 4,500 frames per second at each of the string tensions shown in Table 2-1 (40 lb, 50 lb, 60 lb, and 70 lb) to see how long the ball stayed on the strings. Table 2-2 shows that a ball stays on the strings longer at the lower string tension. But what does this have to do with control?

Here's one explanation of what might happen: An increase in string tension causes the ball to be *flattened out* during impact. This flattening

TABLE 2-2   The Effects of String Tension on Contact Duration

Tension (lb)	Contact Duration (ms)
40	4.08
50	4.07
60	4.05
70	3.82

out, in turn, causes an *embedding* of the strings into the nap of the tennis ball. The greater the embedding of the ball, the greater the control. A second explanation might stem from the fact that a trampoline effect occurs at lower string tensions and that the ball is on the racquet face longer. Therefore, when a ball is hit off-center (as most are) the racquet has more time to rotate in reaction to the impact and send the ball off in an errant direction.

In deciding what string to use you should consider what your personal needs are. Table 2-3 might help.

As for deciding what string tension to use, think about what your game style is like? Do you need a bit more velocity or more control on your shots? When deciding, be sure not to sacrifice one for the other. A balanced combination is optimum for most people.

THE GRIP SIZE

One more factor exists that you must take into consideration before buying your new racquet: the correct grip size. This is a serious component of racquet selection that is often overlooked by skilled players. They always try a couple of grip sizes that feel good and then usually select the

TABLE 2-3   A Comparison of Gut and Synthetic String

	Gut	Synthetic
Cost	More expensive	Less expensive
Durability	Less	More
Affected by humidity and dampness	More	Less
Life span	Shorter	Longer
Resiliency	More	Less
Control	More	Less
Ball velocity	Higher	Lower
Vibration levels	Lower	Higher

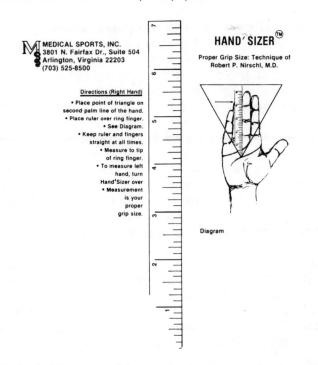

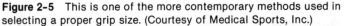

Figure 2-5 This is one of the more contemporary methods used in selecting a proper grip size. (Courtesy of Medical Sports, Inc.)

smaller grip size because of the *whippy* feeling the racquet gives them. This is a dangerous practice for one very simple reason: The smaller the grip size, the tighter you must squeeze the handle to maintain racquet control at impact. The tighter the racquet is squeezed, the more your hand becomes fixed to the racquet. The more your hand becomes fixed to the racquet, the greater the transmission of force from the racquet to the hand, wrist, forearm, and elbow. Therefore, if you are a player who likes the whippy feeling provided by a smaller grip, you may be asking for trouble. To determine the proper grip size for you, one of the most commonly accepted methods is to measure the distance from the middle palm line of the hand to the end of your ring finger (Figure 2-5).

YOUR TENNIS SHOES AND YOU

When you purchase a pair of tennis shoes, what factors do you consider? Everyone is aware of their specific shoe size, the style they want, and the comfort they want. However, what entails a perfect shoe fit for a tennis player? Besides fitting the structure of your foot, what about your style of play? Should it affect your shoe selection? Do you consider what court surface you play on and how your choice might affect your performance? The skilled tennis player must confront these questions when purchasing tennis shoes. The shoes you select will not only affect your quality of play but they may also dictate how long you'll play the game.

Few people realize that the average person takes almost 20,000 steps per day and that with each step, a force of about 120% of the body's weight is transmitted through the foot to the ground. Imagine the enormous percentages of body weight encountered when running. Then consider what these numbers become for the quick starts and stops required in tennis. Consider that the foot contains some 26 bones along with tiny muscles and a mass of connective tissue. Slam all of that into the ground for three hours a day on the practice court and it's no wonder a skilled tennis player may have sore feet.

The footwork required in tennis is unlike that in most other sports: quick starts in all directions, quick stops from all directions, jumping at different angles (e.g., straight up vs. angled backward), landing and twisting (Figure 2-6). This myriad of maneuvers is further complicated by: (1) the existence of approximately 16 different tennis court surfaces, (2) various climatic conditions (e.g., weather and humidity levels), and (3) dramatic court surface temperature changes relative to altitude, climate, and season. All of these factors may affect the friction (traction) between a shoe and surface.

Your Game Style

Let's first consider style of play in your selection of a tennis shoe. Many players are baseliners, whether they hit relentless offensive ground strokes or they like to retrieve and hit moonballs. These players' feet, ob-

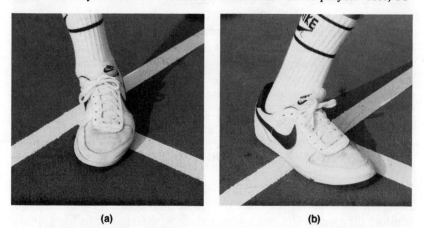

(a)   (b)

Figure 2-6(a),(b) These photos depict some of the various foot movements involved in tennis.

Figure 2-7   Imagine the lateral forces at the foot that are involved as a skilled player pushes off toward one side.

viously, encounter a great deal of lateral (to the outside) and medial (to the inside) forces as they push off sideways for a shot or try to catch themselves and change direction (Figure 2-7). This is not to say they shouldn't worry about forward (anterior) or rear (posterior) forces, but their major support needs will be in the side walls of a shoe. The serve-and-volley player also exerts a great deal of side wall force in pushing off to volley, but this player will also generate very high levels of forward forces into the shoe's toe box when approaching the net (Figure 2-8). If a serve-and-volleyer wears a shoe that doesn't fit properly, it's possible for the foot to slide forward in the shoe and cause what is known as black toe: a discoloration of the toe due to bruising.

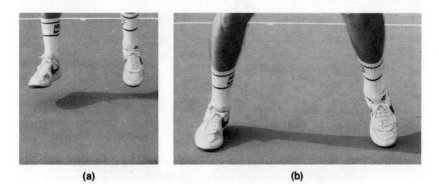

(a)   (b)

Figure 2-8(a),(b)   Imagine the forward forces encountered by this individual's toes if these shoes did not fit properly when performing this movement.

Court Surface

Another external factor besides style of play may affect your decision in selecting a tennis shoe: the court surface. How the shoe sole interacts with the court surface could definitely dictate your caliber of play. For example, if you were playing on a hard court and were wearing shoes designed to slide on clay you might not be able to change directions quickly enough, which would risk your safety, moreover what it would do to your game.

The traction between a shoe sole and court surface has generated great controversy. The next time you are in a shoe store, look at the soles of various tennis shoes. You may see wavy lines, z-patterned lines, concentric circles, uneven circular projections, or combinations of these sole patterns (Figure 2-9). The problem is that little independent research has been conducted to determine what is best for a particular surface. Some manufacturers tailor shoe soles to specific court surfaces, so be sure to read the company's literature to be sure your shoe meets your needs.

Shoe Construction

Through the analysis of high-speed films, it has been determined that most foot striking patterns in tennis involve heel strike (regardless of skill level), the movement of force along the lateral aspect of the shoe sole, and the transmission of that force across to the ball of the foot (Figure 2-10). This reveals several things to the prospective buyer of the shoe. First, the construction of the heel cup should be near to form fitting; it should be snug but not constricting (Figure 2-11). This prevents the foot from slipping out of the shoe and also helps to distribute impact forces more evenly. Second, a snug heel cup seems to be the most important factor in preventing the foot from sliding forward inside the shoe. Also,

Figure 2-9 Here you can see some of the tennis shoe sole patterns seen on the market today.

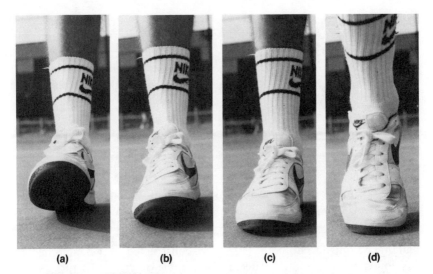

| **(a)** | **(b)** | **(c)** | **(d)** |

Figure 2-10(a),(b),(c),(d) This slow-motion sequence shows how forces are transmitted along a shoe sole.

a rounded outer heel seems to be more beneficial than a square heel construction. The square heel may cause the foot to actually slap the ground after going over the edges, but a round heel allows the foot to make contact in a smoother and more controlled manner. A soft, pliable, molded heel will also absorb shock better.

Figure 2-11 This is one of the common methods of testing the fit of your shoe's heel cup.

Figure 2-12 Notice the two materials used to make the sole of this shoe.

Shoe soles must cushion and endure! Some shoes are made from a material designed to do both. Others are constructed of two materials: a cushioned midsole and a harder, more durable outer sole (Figure 2-12). Dr. Robert Simpson (1982), a podiatrist in Alton, IL, and a former college varsity tennis player, feels that a polyurethane sole of two thicknesses (a spongy white inner sole and a pliable, but more firm, outer sole of polyurethane composition) is best. To go a step further, Nike has begun to incorporate into their tennis shoes an air sole that will provide even more cushioning. With proper support and cushioning in this area, the likelihood of foot, lower leg, and knee trauma will be lessened.

Shock absorption and support continue from the heel area through the midfoot. To test for midfoot flexibility, flex the sole in the middle (Figure 2-13). Try to avoid the two extremes: a stiff shoe and a shoe that is too pliable. Too much rigidity absorbs little shock while too much pliability provides little support. This flexion test, though simple, can reveal striking differences among shoe styles.

The force of foot impact moves through the midfoot to the

Figure 2-13 This is a recommended test for shoe flexibility.

Figure 2-14 This pivoting action performed by Tim Gullikson gives one an idea of the forces encountered by the shoe sole under the ball of the foot.

forefoot. Since the body is beginning its push-off and may be twisting over the forefoot to change direction, this area of shoe design is crucial. The greatest pressure may be over the ball of the foot so you should examine how well that area of the shoe sole is reinforced. In Figure 2-14 you can see what happens at the ball of the foot as Tim Gullikson maneuvers to hit a shot. Again, this area should not be too rigid, because a great deal of force is encountered in the forefoot. That force could traumatize the foot if poorly distributed and absorbed.

Finally, are you a toe dragger? When you finish serving are there long white lines behind the baseline (Figure 2-15) caused by what used to

(a)   (b)

Figure 2-15(a),(b) In part (a), you can see how many players drag their toe with the trail foot while serving. In part (b), you can view the white lines commonly seen behind the baseline of many tennis courts. These lines are caused by the toe of a player's tennis shoe.

be part of your shoe? One player on the tour even drags the top of his shoe during ground strokes and goes through the upper before any sign of wear appears on the sole. Not only does this ruin a pair of tennis shoes prematurely, dragging your toe can also affect your balance and your timing. If you drag your toe the best solution is to take some footwork lessons and get out of the habit! It might save you money in the long run. The next best answer, however, is to purchase a shoe with a reinforced toe. Look for shoes with very sturdy outer soles. Several shoe styles even have a larger than usual toe, usually reinforced with polyurethane or some other synthetic. This added padding will help the shoes last a little longer, but the shoe still will probably die before its time.

Selecting a Tennis Shoe

Up to this point, we've discussed shoe selection according to style of play, court surface, support and cushioning of the foot, as well as wearability. Little has been said regarding basic foot structure and its involvement in shoe selection. I will refer back to my work with Dr. Simpson and relate his expertise in podiatry with my study of biomechanics.

Everyone knows their shoe size. When trying on a pair of shoes, we all stand up, lean over, and push the front of the shoe in to determine how much room our toes have. This is a good indicator of the amount of space available in the toe box. You don't want a toe box that constricts, nor do you want a shoe with an oversized toe box that permits free forward migration of the foot. An easy test for this is to stand on the store's carpet and force your foot forward in the shoe. This should indicate how you'll feel later during a tennis match.

Foot width also affects arch support and force distribution. A good rule of thumb while trying on a pair of shoes is to lace both securely, stand up, and let your weight sway to the inside over the arch and then to the outside over the side (Figure 2-16). If you feel too much pressure from the shoe's own arch, or if you feel any pinching, the shoe's probably too tight; too much foot motion within the shoe may not support your arch adequately and too much pronation (turning outward) of the foot can cause severe lower leg and knee trauma.

The heel cup of a shoe should be snug to the foot but not restricting. If it's too tight you may have problems with force distribution and bruising, and if it's too loose, foot control will be poor and blisters may develop. Also, test where the top inner edge of the heel cup contacts your foot. Some people blister easily if the shoe's edge rubs too much against the rear of the foot. If you blister easily, prevention of the problem is the best cure you could have.

In the end, it seems that the old adage, "If the shoe fits, wear it," may not necessarily be right. It's how the shoe fits that affects your play

Figure 2-16 This is the recommended action for testing the lateral and medial stability of a tennis shoe.

and the amount of time you can spend on the court. When you select a pair of tennis shoes, bear the following in mind:

- All tennis players need foot support, but do you have any specific needs based on:
  1. your foot structure,
  2. your style of play, or
  3. the court surface you play on.

Consideration of these factors could have a positive effect on how well you play and how long you play but, better yet, it will allow you to fit your shoe to you.

SO MANY DIFFERENT TENNIS BALLS: WHY?

I thought it was very interesting when the two-tone orange and yellow tennis balls hit the market. They were advertised as being 23% easier to see and were to make a big improvement in your game. However, they never said anything about your opponent also being able to see the ball 23% better and how his or her game would also improve.

Tennis balls are a big part of the market. In 1975, for instance, the tennis ball industry accounted for approximately 20% of the total money spent by the tennis consumer in the United States. Because that part of the industry is so profitable, many brands of tennis balls exist. Their selection may depend on the court surface to be played on, the altitude, the duration of play, or the ball color you like. Most tennis players acknowledge that there is a difference among the various brand names of tennis balls on the market. The differences range from variations in flight and rebound characteristics to the ball's ability to maintain constant characteristics during play (e.g., whether they *fluff up* or not). Let's discuss some of these differences.

One major identifying characteristic among some brands of tennis balls is whether they are pressurized or not. Nonpressurized balls may be useful at higher altitudes but you will seldom see them used at major tournaments. The reason is that many skilled players say they feel like rocks when they hit the racquet. Some authorities even feel that the impact is so heavy that use of these balls could hurt your arm. Little research has been conducted on the nonpressurized ball so none of this information can be verified, but you should be aware that most advanced players prefer playing with pressurized tennis balls.

Once a tennis ball is pressurized, it must be placed in a vacuum sealed container so each ball will maintain its pressure. You can tell if the can was properly sealed because when opened it makes a short, but loud, hiss. After a pressurized can of balls has been opened each ball will maintain its original rebound characteristics for about a week (Rand, 1979). After a week, the tennis ball will gradually lose its pressure and become dead.

Most pressurized tennis balls are manufactured for use at near sea-level atmospheric conditions. Those of you who have a chance to play in higher altitudes should be aware that high-altitude balls are made by almost all major manufacturers. In fact, if you try to play a match at a mountain resort using sea-level balls, you are in for a frustrating day because the sea-level balls will tend to sail out of bounds. In contrast, don't take the high-altitude balls home with you or to the beach. These tennis balls are specifically made for use in low-pressure altitudes.

When you make a tennis ball purchase, you might read on the can that it contains balls classified as *championship* or *extra duty*. Extra-duty tennis balls have more wool nap on the rubber cover which allows the ball to have a longer life span. The main disadvantage of these balls is that on a clay surface, and on some hard courts, they tend to fluff up and become heavy. Championship balls do not contain as much nap covering and do not fluff up as much. Their main disadvantage is that they won't last as long as some players might like. Most U.S.T.A. tournaments use the championship ball, but you should realize that new balls are introduced at various points in a match because they lose their original characteristics and may become light due to loss of nap.

As you select a tennis ball for competition or practice, consider the court surface and how long you want to use the balls. If you are collecting practice balls, you will probably want to buy extra-duty balls. If you are competing or are practicing on a clay court, you may want to select championship balls.

SUMMARY OF EQUIPMENT SELECTION

Always be selective when buying your tennis equipment. It's easy to be swayed into a purchase by sales people. Don't buy whatever seems to be the most popular brand name. Regardless of the equipment you are looking for, be objective in making your choice. Ask yourself the following questions:

- What are my physical needs (i.e., grip size, foot structure, and so on)?
- Does my style of play affect my equipment needs?
- Could this purchase make me a more effective player?

By being mainly objective in your selection of equipment, you will narrow down the choices that will be best for you. Then you can be more subjective by playtesting the equipment to see how it will feel when you use it. By approaching your purchases in this manner, you will be getting equipment that's better suited to you.

REFERENCES

Blanksby, B., Elliott, B., & Ellis, R. (1979). Selecting the right racquet: Performance characteristics of regular-sized and oversized tennis racquets. *Australian Journal of Health, Physical Education and Recreation*, **86**, 21-25.

Brody, H. (1979). Physics of the tennis racquet. *American Journal of Physics*, **47**(6), 482-487.

Elliott, B., Blanksby, B., & Ellis, R. (1980). Vibrations and rebound velocity characteristics of conventional and oversized tennis racquets. *Research Quarterly for Exercise and Sport*, **51**, 608-615.

Rand, K.T., Hyer, M.W., & Williams, M.H. (1979). A dynamic test for comparison of rebound characteristics of three brands of tennis balls. In J. Groppel (Ed.), *Proceedings of the National Symposium on the Racquet Sports*, University of Illinois Conferences and Institutes.

Simpson, R.R. (1982). Foot and lower leg problems in racquet sport athletes. In J. Groppel (Ed.), *Proceedings of the Fourth International Symposium on the Effective Teaching of Racquet Sports*. University of Illinois Conferences and Institutes, 33-35.

Other Recommended Readings

An, B. (1979). A theoretical model of a physiologically natural grip for racquets in racquet sports. In J. Groppel (Ed.), *Proceedings of a National Symposium on the Racquet Sports*. University of Illinois at Urbana-Champaign, Conferences and Institutes.

Baker, J., & Putnam, C. (1979). Tennis racket and ball responses during impact under clamped and freestanding conditions. *Research Quarterly*, **50**, 164-170.

Braden, V., & Bruns, B. (1977). *Tennis for the Future*. Boston: Little, Brown and Co.

Brody, H. (1981). Physics of the tennis racket II: The "sweet spot." *American Journal of Physics*, **49**(9), 816-819.

Broer, M., & Zernicke, R. (1979). *Efficiency of Human Movement*. Philadelphia: W.B. Saunders.

Bunn, J. (1972). *Scientific Principles of Coaching*. Englewood Cliffs, N.J.: Prentice-Hall, Inc.

Cochan, A., and Stobbs, J. (1968). *Search for the Perfect Swing*. New York: J.B. Lippincott.

Daish, C.B. (1972). *Learn Science Through Ball Games*. London: English Universities Press.

Elliott, B., and Kilderry, R. (1983). *The Art and Science of Tennis*. Philadelphia: Saunders College Publishing.

Groppel, J. (1983). Gut reactions. *World Tennis*, **31**(6), 28-30.

Hatze, H. (1976). Forces and duration of impact, and grip tightness during the tennis stroke. *Medicine and Science in Sports*, **8**, 88-95.

Murphy, B., and Murphy, C. (1975). *Tennis for the Player, Teacher and Coach*. Philadelphia: W.B. Saunders.

Plagenhoef, S. (1971). *Patterns of Human Motion: A Cinematographical Analysis*. Englewood Cliffs, N.J.: Prentice-Hall, Inc.

Plagenhoef, S. (1970). *Fundamentals of Tennis*. Englewood Cliffs, N.J.: Prentice-Hall, Inc.

Plagenhoef, S. (1979). Tennis racquet testing related to "tennis elbow." In J. Groppel (Ed.), *Proceedings of a National Symposium on the Racquet Sports*. University of Illinois at Urbana-Champaign, Division of Conferences and Institutes.

Tilmanis, Gundars A. (1975). *Advanced Tennis for Coaches, Teachers and Players*. Philadelphia: Lea and Febiger.

Watanabe, T., Ikegami, Y., & Miyashita, M. (1979). Tennis: The effects of grip firmness on ball velocity after impact. *Medicine and Science in Sports*, **11**, 359-361.

Footwork's
the Name
of the Game

GLOSSARY

Closed Stance — Used when the player steps across with the foot opposite the side where the ball will be hit.

Friction — Caused by opposing contact forces from two different surfaces (e.g., your tennis shoes and the court).

Open Stance — Used when the player steps toward the sideline with the foot on the same side as where the ball is located.

Recovery Step — Occurs following impact when the trail leg comes around with the follow-through.

Unit Turn — The initial footwork and body rotation that should occur as you prepare for a stroke.

Unweighting — The reduction of force between your feet and the tennis court.

Anyone who has taken tennis lessons knows of the emphasis placed on footwork and body positioning. The rationale for this should be obvious since body movement is a necessity for competing at the elite level. However, as some players become skilled they tend to emphasize stroke production more than body positioning. I understand why these tennis players feel this way, but their priorities may be a bit confused. In my opinion, footwork is one of the most important, yet most overlooked, aspects of championship tennis. Few athletes completely understand the role of a ready position, unweighting to move, or how to time a shot that has to be hit on the run. In fact, when a player misses a crucial shot the fault usually lies, not in the stroke itself, but in the footwork.

PREPARATION STANCE AND UNWEIGHTING

Good footwork begins with a ready position: slightly bent knees, weight forward on the balls of the feet, bent slightly forward at the waist (moving one's center of gravity lower and more forward than normal), and the racquet held directly in front of the body. In this position the player is ready to move with equal quickness in all directions. Although the ready-position stance is fairly well accepted, it has recently come under some fire. Other authorities prefer to use a more generalized preparatory stance called a *neutral position.*

The neutral position doesn't really describe any one particular stance. Since the knees bend to move regardless of whether you are bent lower or not, these advocates ask "why bend down prematurely?" They feel that a player should merely be aware of the opponent's shot. If aware of the opponent's stroke, the player will read the shot just as well and move with the same or greater quickness than a player who assumes a ready position. Figure 3-1 should give you an idea of the various ways to assume a ready position. These athletes are all aware of the opponent's movements but await his/her shot differently. From this it would seem that the controversy on the ready position deserves further discussion of the mechanical concepts involved.

Regardless of the position a skilled tennis player assumes while awaiting the opponent's shot, upon or just prior to impact by the opponent the player will unweight. (This is the same term you may have heard used to describe how a snow skier shifts his or her weight to turn.) Unweighting refers to a lessening of the frictional force between a competitor's shoes and the court surface as demonstrated in Figure 3-2. Before an athlete prepares to move toward a shot, for example, the force of his/her shoes against the court is equal to his/her body weight. Once a decision is made to move, the knees flex quickly. During this rapid knee flexion the force of the athlete's body on the court surface lowers considerably and then, during knee extension, it increases significantly to create a large force against the ground. To see how this works, stand on your bathroom scale and note the reading. Now jump off the scale. You will see the needle deflecting in two directions. First, it will drop below your actual weight (for a very short time) and then go above it. This is exactly what happens in a ski turn and when preparing to run for a tennis

(a) (b)

Figure 3-1(a), (b) These athletes demonstrate their personal preferences on how to assume a ready position.

shot. Therefore, regardless of which preparatory stance you use, both require unweighting to occur so the feet can get oriented properly and the first application of force from the feet to the ground can be accomplished correctly.

Figure 3-2 The author demonstrates how a tennis player unweights. Observe the knee flexion and ankle movement to quickly lower the center of gravity.

(a)   (b)   (c)

Figure 3-3(a), (b), (c) This athlete illustrates how to correctly move
to return an opponent's shot. Notice how the unweighting acts to
prepare her for movement into the stroke's preparation.

You can see the importance of unweighting the next time you are
watching a televised tennis match. First of all, observe the position a
player assumes just as the opponent serves the ball. It's usually not the
classic ready position that everyone visualizes in their mind. Skilled
players will go through some sort of a footwork routine just to stay loose
while awaiting the opponent's shot. But as the opponent hits the ball an
athlete will take a slight hop forward, as you see in Figure 3-3. This acts
to set the leg muscles for the return, but more importantly, notice how
the player's center of gravity (denoted by the hips) shifts downward. This
ballistic lowering of the center of gravity is the unweighting and is usually
timed according to when the performer anticipates how he or she must
move to hit the ball.

Also, try to focus on one player during a point and watch how he/
she moves between shots. Regardless of the movement, you should almost always be able to detect the unweighting as he or she quickly lowers
the center of gravity and pushes off. Be aware, however, that the lowering of the body is slight and may be difficult to see.

THE UNIT TURN

Once you've unweighted for a shot, the next movement that usually occurs is the *unit turn*. The unit turn has become popular just recently.
Therefore, a majority of tennis players have never been introduced to it.
For example, before you heard step into the ball from your teacher you
were most likely told to get your racquet back as soon as the ball is seen

coming off the opponent's racquet. This statement has to be among the most popular instructional cues ever used. However, there is a lot more to stroke preparation than merely getting the racquet back. It's all in the feet, as described by Don Usher and David Fish, two tennis coaches from Harvard University. They studied the footwork of professional tennis players for several years and observed a common motion they call the unit turn.

What's involved in a unit turn is this: From your ready stance, as soon as you recognize the side of your body to which the opponent's shot will be coming, you move the foot closest to the ball outward as you see in Figure 3-4. For example, if the ball is coming to a righthander's forehand, the right foot should be picked up and moved slightly to the right so that it is pointing to the side. As this happens, the whole right side of the body, including the racquet, should rotate around to the right. Doing this will also create a slight forward imbalance. Although it is desirable to step toward the ball with the opposite foot, the unit turn allows for the stroke to be hit regardless of whether or not you have time to step into the shot. However, if you don't step into the shot there is a tendency to be lazy, causing your center of gravity to remain either directly above or behind your feet (instead of slightly ahead as it should) and you may hit the ball poorly.

Because the unit turn naturally involves motion to the side, it readily prepares the body for quick lateral movement. It enhances lateral mo-

(a)   (b)

Figure 3-4(a), (b) Tim Mayotte demonstrates the unit turn to the forehand side (a) and when using a backhand (b) to return a ball served at his body.

Figure 3-5(a), (b), (c), (d) This athlete demonstrates how to move quickly to the side. Notice the shuffling of the feet (parts a, b, and c) which allows him to move more rapidly than using a complete striding movement.

tion in two different ways: shuffling the feet sideways or sprinting. First, imagine that the ball is only going to be about 6 feet directly to your right at impact (see Figure 3-5). You may not have to sprint, but you will still need to move quickly. In explaining how to do this, I like to use an analogy from basketball. Picture Larry Bird of the Boston Celtics playing defense near the basket about 5 feet from his own baseline. He is guarding an opposing player who has the ball. His opponent begins to drive the baseline against him. How will Bird cut off the guard from driving around him? Obviously, he won't sprint 5 feet. He will "slide" over to the baseline, cutting off the opponent's path to the basket. This sliding,

(a)	(b)	(c)

Figure 3-6(a), (b), (c)   Here you can see the body mechanics used when sprinting toward a shot. Notice the unit turn (in part b) to begin the sprint and how the racquet arm is used in a "pumping" action.

as you see the athlete doing in Figure 3-5, is accomplished by shuffling the feet side to side very quickly. It's the quickest way to move sideways for a short distance.

When you have to sprint for a return, the unit turn best prepares you to run. When the foot fires out to the side, as shown in Figure 3-6, it tips your body in the desired direction faster. To correct this imbalance, your opposite foot crosses over and you're immediately in a running position.

HITTING ON THE RUN

Skilled players must be able to hit a shot on the run. While being a crowd pleaser in itself, one of the most exhilarating feelings in tennis is to be running full tilt and hit a down-the-line passing shot for a clear winner. However, even as it is thrilling, that shot has to be one of the toughest in tennis because of the required footwork, body positioning, timing, and racquet work necessary to make it successful.

The key point to remember about hitting on the run is to be as balanced as possible. Sometimes body stability is very difficult to master, especially if the opponent continually hits short or angled shots. In situations like this, hitting on the run is often a must and balance is the least of a player's worries. However, many times a player will hit a shot on the run when there was no need to hit the ball like that. Whether it's laziness, poor timing, inaccurate awareness of the ball off the opponent's racquet, or just the desire to hit crowd pleasers, many shots hit on the run don't

(a)   (b)

(c)   (d)

Figure 3-7(a), (b), (c), (d)   Sometimes you will be forced to hit on the run, but many players perform as seen here. This athlete is timing his *body* to the point of impact (instead of timing his stroke to the point of impact) which causes a hurried swing.

have to be. When you watch a player who seems to be hitting a great number of balls while sprinting (as the player in Figure 3-7 is doing), watch his/her footwork and body positioning. Their footwork might be a little lazy, even slow-motion, at the start of their movement toward the ball. Then as the ball gets closer to where contact will occur, the player suddenly increases speed and ends up lurching at the ball. Players who do this are timing their body to the position of ball contact and not their stroke, making a balanced shot almost impossible. This causes a hurried, cramped swing that often has poor results. To correct this problem, a competitor needs to get to the court position where the ball will be hit *before* the ball gets there. The player in Figure 3-8 shows that when you arrive early at the site of ball contact stability will be easier to achieve as will the timing and accuracy of the stroke.

If a ball must be hit on the run, how can a player do it most effectively? To get to the position of ball contact rapidly, as shown in Figure 3-9, a sprinting person must use their arms. The arms assist in coordinating the quick acceleration of the legs. The racquet arm can be held

(a)   (b)

(c)   (d)

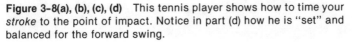

Figure 3-8(a), (b), (c), (d)   This tennis player shows how to time your *stroke* to the point of impact. Notice in part (d) how he is "set" and balanced for the forward swing.

in close just the same as it would be when sprinting without the racquet. The key is knowing when the racquet leaves the rhythmic motion of running to initiate the backswing. Many players go through total dysfunction when trying to combine all these movements. To be the most balanced performer possible, the opposing limbs should move in synchrony (i.e., left leg and right arm). Picture sprinting to the side to hit a forehand passing shot down the line. Try to run slightly forward, as this player (Figure 3-9) illustrates, so your linear momentum will be toward the point of impact. As the foot nearest the net contacts the ground, the racquet arm moves into its slightly circular backswing. The swing continues and, as the hind foot pushes off the ground, the hips and trunk rotate slightly, transferring that ground reaction force to the racquet arm for an effective ball contact well in front of the body. There are obviously other ways to hit a ball on the run, but this will allow the total use of linear and angular body momentum. The timing for certain shots may not permit this movement coordination either, but if time and body positioning allow, this would be the most efficient.

(a)   (b)   (c)

(d)   (e)

Figure 3-9(a), (b), (c), (d), (e)   There will be times when you are forced to hit a shot on the run. This competitor shows how to sprint using the arms (parts a and b) and to hit on the run by moving *forward* into the shot.

RETURNING A BALL HIT RIGHT AT YOU

Just as some people have trouble hitting a ball on the run, there are others who seem to have a phobia for balls coming right at them. They often panic and simply don't know what to do. This occurs most often at the beginning level of tennis, but it can also be seen at the skilled level. Some players standing at the baseline will recognize the ball coming right at them and, seemingly unaware of what should happen next, they scoop the racquet in front to keep the ball in play. This embarrassing situation is the result of poor concentration and less than perfect footwork.

Two means of footwork can be employed to better position yourself for a ball headed straight at you. The pros are usually the best at the

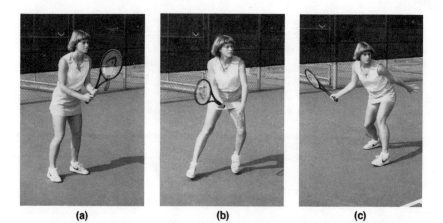

(a)   **(b)**   **(c)**

Figure 3-10(a), (b), (c)   Observe how a skilled tennis player will hop
to anticipate and *immediately* move forward into the shot.

first maneuver. They will keep their footwork continuous during a point
and once they recognize the ball traveling towards them, they will hop to
the side into position for the return (see Figure 3-10). Moving to the side
quickly, they maintain their center of gravity over their feet to stay in
balance and can hit their normal stroke. This is where less skilled competitors run into trouble. How far to the side do you hop? If the movement is too far, you have to lunge at the ball when you swing and, if your
motion isn't far enough, the swing will be hurried and cramped. Experience at doing this is important but it doesn't take too much practice
to learn the hopping action. If you have a problem with it, you can start
by using the second method of moving your body out of the ball's flight
path.

The second method is slower than the hopping movement and can
be used during slow rallies — but it should only be used as a means of improving your body positioning so you can graduate to the first method.
The motion somewhat resembles a dance step as demonstrated in Figure
3-11. As soon as the ball is recognized as coming right at you, side step
with the foot opposite where the ball is traveling. Your next move is to
pivot about that foot backward and behind. This motion removes you
from the path of the ball, makes you aware of how far out of the way
you need to be to hit effectively, and still helps you maintain a stable base
of support for the stroke. As your hind foot touches the court, prepare to
push forward on it (depending how fast the ball is approaching) and step
into the shot with the opposite foot. Again, this is an optimal movement
for slow rallies but, because of its time demands, it cannot be easily
employed in competition. However, it should serve to help you advance
to the first method which is much quicker and more conducive to highly
skilled performance.

(a)   **(b)**   **(c)**

Figure 3-11(a), (b), (c) This is the dance step action you can use when you don't have to hurry to hit a shot.

THE RECOVERY STEP

Once a skilled tennis player has gotten into the proper position for a shot, his/her hind leg is often seen coming around during the follow-through, making the body almost square to the net (Figure 3-12). Connors, McEnroe, and Vilas do this quite often. As these players hit a ground stroke, it is not uncommon to see their trail leg come around during the follow-through, become planted to the side of the body, and push off to return to the center of the baseline.

(a)   **(b)**

Figure 3-12(a), (b) Here you can see how the recovery step takes place. Notice in part b how the hind leg has swung around *following impact* to permit the player to use a push-off in returning toward the center of the court.

If you are to enter the elite levels of competition, you must eventually master the recovery step. The high velocities of most ground strokes actually force the body to rotate toward a recovery step maneuver. The problem is doing it in a controlled manner. Sequence is everything; if you try the recovery step too soon in the process of hitting a ball, you'll botch the shot.

As you begin to develop a recovery step in your stroking movements, be aware that the step isn't necessary on every shot you hit. It becomes effective on wide shots that you are forced to retrieve or when you must run for a return. In each of these instances, the recovery step will assist you in returning to an optimal center court position.

Before trying to perform the recovery step, remember that shot control is your first priority. When employing the recovery step, first be sure your stroke imparts the direction and pace you want when you hit the ball. Then, when fully aware that contact has occurred and the ball has left your racquet, you can pull your trail leg around into the neutral, or ready, position and push off to return to the desired position on the court. Be sure, however, that you don't try the recovery step too soon in your stroke. An attempt to recover too early will open your body stance during the swing and cause a very poor shot. Take it slow at first to develop the proper timing. Once you gain the appropriate coordination, the recovery step can be an important tool in your game.

OPEN- AND CLOSED-STANCE GROUND STROKES

Many players don't need to worry about a recovery step because they are often already *opened up* when they hit the ball. There are many theories, both positive and negative, about open-stance ground strokes. As a rule, there's nothing wrong with an open-stance stroke, provided the player has time to get set and hit the ball correctly. There are only certain strokes, however, that allow usage of an open stance. For example, have you ever wondered why the forehand is so often hit with an open stance, as Brian Gottfried demonstrates in Figure 3-13? How often do you see a one-handed backhand hit from an open stance? Let's analyze these various ground strokes to determine some answers.

If a right-handed player stands facing the net awaiting the opponent's shot and the opponent strikes a ball toward his forehand side, the player may only have to side step and swing; hence, the open-stance forehand. There will be little transfer of body weight forward; only body rotation will allow the athlete to take a sufficient backswing and swing effectively. This will be discussed in depth in the next chapter.

However, seldom will you see a one-handed backhand hit from an open stance. Notice this right-handed player at the baseline facing the

Figure 3-13 Observe the body positioning for Brian Gottfried's open-stance forehand drive.

net. If a ball is hit to the player's backhand (or left) side, the racquet is on the opposite side of the body from the position of the ball (Figure 3-14). Therefore, he must reach across his body to prepare the racquet for the return. Imagine the contortions he would have to go through to side step toward the ball and hit an open-stance, one-handed backhand (Figure 3-15). Therefore, I recommend you use the orthodox, closed-stance, one-handed backhand seen in Figure 3-16. As may be evident, good footwork is essential to adequately position your body sideways for the stroke.

Figure 3-14 Observe how this athlete's swinging limb is on the opposite side of where impact must occur.

Figure 3-15 This player demonstrates why an open-stance one-handed backhand is difficult to hit. Observe how his hips are completely open toward the net but his trunk must go through a severe contortion to accomplish a backswing. Although it is possible to hit this stroke, it is unlikely that a player could be very effective.

Footwork is also necessary for a successful two-handed backhand, but what about an open-stance two-hander? You will actually see more open-stance, two-handed backhands than one-handers, but why? One reason may come from some of the coaching literature of the 1970s when the two-handed backhand became so popular. Many of the authors re-

(a)   (b)   (c)

Figure 3-16(a), (b), (c) This tennis player demonstrates the proper movements when hitting an effective one-handed backhand drive.

Figure 3-17 This figure drawing of Bjorn Borg (taken from films shot at 100 frames per second) shows how he hit his effective half-open stance two-handed backhand drive so well.

ferred to the two-handed backhand (of a right-handed player) as being similar to hitting a left-handed forehand. They implied that since the left hand was placed closer to the racquet face, it was the more important of the two hands. Whether you believe this rationale or not, it may help to explain the possibility of hitting the two-handed backhand with an open stance. Saying that the stroke resembles a left-handed forehand (of a right-handed player) implies that the left hand is the dominant producer of force to swing the racquet. That would mean that the body could be open to swing the racquet as long as the right hand was still holding the racquet as a minor producer of force and for additional racquet control. An effective two-hander can be hit so it looks like the stroke was hit with an open stance. As you can see from Figure 3-17, some players will set up to swing in a half-open stance (stepping more toward the net instead of directly toward the ball) and, as they initiate the swing, their trunk will rotate toward the ball along with a recovery step, which makes it seem like the player has actually swung with a completely open stance.

SUMMARY

No matter how unique or spectacular you think an open stance ground stroke is, most players should always try to get into position as quickly as possible and step into the shot. This method helps to improve footwork and to hit with better control. The player who steps into the shot will also be able to reach further with more control; the player using the open-stance stroke must either get slightly closer to the ball for an effective impact or move quicker to get in position for the swing. Sometimes, however, there isn't time to stop and step into the shot; the open-stance shot may be all you have.

Regardless of whether you prefer open- or closed-stance shots, there are several things to remember when working on your body positioning. As you await the opponent's shot, try to keep your feet moving so that you don't get caught flat-footed. I tell my players to have "happy feet" as they get prepared for a return. When the opponent begins his or her forward swing, take a very short hop to set your leg muscles for movement to the ball. This hop should be timed so that you land at exactly the same time the opponent hits the ball. Your first movement should then be a unit turn to the side. If you don't have to sprint for the ball, shuffle your feet and get prepared as early as possible. If you must sprint toward the ball, try to get there early so you can be as stable as possible. Avoid hitting on the run whenever you can.

As far as hitting with an open or closed stance, you can do whatever you want. Remember, however, that most players don't hit from an open stance because it might be more effective, but simply because they're lazy. If you're one of these individuals, the next chapter will teach you how to use your entire body to hit a more effective ground stroke. For those who already step into the ball, I'd advise you also to continue reading. Someday you might be hitting an open-stance forehand just like everyone else — we're all a little lazy!

RECOMMENDED READINGS

Braden, V., & Bruns, B. (1977). *Tennis for the Future*. Boston: Little, Brown and Co.

Broer, M., & Zernicke, R. (1979). *Efficiency of Human Movement*. Philadelphia: W.B. Saunders.

Bunn, J. (1972). *Scientific Principles of Coaching*. Englewood Cliffs, N.J.: Prentice-Hall, Inc.

Cochan, A., and Stobbs, J. (1968). *Search for the Perfect Swing*. New York: J.B. Lippincott.

Daish, C.B. (1972). *Learn Science Through Ball Games*. London: English Universities Press.

Gonzales, P., and Hyams, J. (1974). *Winning tactics for weekend singles*. New York: Bantam Books.

Groppel, J.L. (1983). Teaching one- and two-handed backhand drives: Biomechanical considerations. *Journal of Physical Education and Recreation*, **54**(5), 23-26.

Hensley, L.D., and Norton, C. (1980). Success in tennis: Keep the ball in play. In J. Groppel (Ed.), *Proceedings of the International Symposium on the Effective Teaching of Racquet Sports*. University of Illinois at Urbana-Champaign, Conferences and Institutes.

Johnson, J., and Xanthos, P. (1967). *Tennis*. Dubuque, IA: Wm. C. Brown Publishers.

Murphy, B., and Murphy, C. (1975). *Tennis for the Player, Teacher and Coach*. Philadelphia: W.B. Saunders.

Nickerson, E. (1982). *Racquet Sports: An Illustrated Guide*. Jefferson, NC: McFarland and Co.

Plagenhoef, S. (1971). *Patterns of Human Motion*. Englewood Cliffs, N.J.: Prentice-Hall, Inc.

Plagenhoef, S. (1970). *Fundamentals of Tennis*. Englewood Cliffs, N.J.: Prentice-Hall, Inc.

Tilmanis, Gundars A. (1975). *Advanced Tennis for Coaches, Teachers and Players*. Philadelphia: Lea and Febiger.

Van der Meer, D. (1982). *Dennis Van der Meer's Complete Book of Tennis*. Norwalk, CT: Golf Digest/Tennis, Inc., New York Times Co.

CHAPTER **4**

Control
Versus Power

GLOSSARY

Angular Momentum — The force generated by body rotation.

Centrifugal Force — The force that radiates outward from the center of a rotating object (i.e., the racquet being pulled away from your body as you swing).

Linear Momentum — The transfer of body weight in a straight line forward in the direction of the shot.

Linked System (kinetic chain) — The successive integration of body segment velocities to generate optimal force for a tennis stroke.

Solid (heavy) Ball — A high-velocity shot that is very penetrating to the opponent.

The correct usage of control and power is probably the single most important factor that separates the great players from the good players. An elite tennis player knows how to mix high-velocity shots with controlled shots. They instinctively know how hard to swing in certain situations to produce the best results. In short, they hit every ball with a purpose, using an optimal combination of force and control when competing.

As a player desiring to improve your competitive level, what should you strive for? How can you best achieve stroke consistency and mix it with the power necessary to perform well in high-level tournaments? The answers to these questions will be discussed in this chapter. However, we first need to differentiate between control and power.

Some authorities define control simply as getting the ball in play as often as possible. Others, a bit more philosophical, say that control in tennis is hitting the last ball of a match over the net and into the opponent's court. Both are good definitions, but the concept of control goes a little deeper. It depends a great deal on the situation at hand. For example, what is control when it's your serve and the score is 4–5 in the third set, 30–40 in the game, and you find yourself on the run for a wide backhand while the opponent is situated about 8 feet from the net ready to pounce on anything you hit? Some competitors might say, "Lob and keep the ball in play. At least make him hit a winner!" Another may think, "I'll go for it; a screamer down the line!" Control for these two players is quite different. The control needed to merely keep the ball in play isn't nearly as difficult as that necessary for the screamer.

Hitting with power doesn't necessarily mean you have to kill the ball to be effective. When you strike a ball with all your might, as a baseball batter might when going for the left-field fence, your body parts are working to generate the highest racquet velocity possible. Your body parts don't care whether the ball makes it over the net or inside the boundaries on the other side; they are only trying to provide the ball with as much impetus as possible. In tennis, you must be concerned about controlling the ball's flight path so that it stays inside the court boundaries yet is penetrating enough to keep the opponent on the defensive. Therefore, hitting with power means that you are optimizing the action between body parts so you can hit a high-velocity stroke and still maintain good control. The pros call this being able to get a "good stick on the ball."

AVOID THOSE COSTLY ERRORS

Keeping the ball in play is, of course, vital. Mistakes are killers! And mistakes occur more often than winners. Many authorities have suggested that more than 75% of all points scored in a match are due to errors. For example, Table 4-1 examines the 1978 NCAA singles final between John McEnroe and John Sadri, and compares the total errors committed and total outright winners made during a four set match that McEnroe won: 7–6 (5–3), 7–6 (5–3), 5–7, 7–6 (5–3). This was an extremely close match with only two points separating winning from losing: 144 points for McEnroe and 142 for Sadri. Note especially that although Sadri served 21 more aces than McEnroe, he also committed 26 more stroking errors. To further emphasize the importance of stroke con-

TABLE 4-1   Match Statistical Summary
94th NCAA Singles Championship*

John McEnroe versus John Sadri
May 29, 1978
Athens, Georgia

	McEnroe	Sadri
Total errors committed	61	87
Forehand	19	30
Backhand	42	57
Crosscourt	29	37
Straight ahead	32	50
Hit from backcourt	47	63
Hit from midcourt	4	10
Hit from net	10	14
Long	14	21
Wide	14	17
Net	30	48
Long and wide	3	1
Double faults	6	8
Total outright winners	46	51
Forehand	28	35
Backhand	18	16
Crosscourt	23	18
Straight ahead	23	33
Hit from backcourt	14	15
Hit from midcourt	6	13
Hit from net	26	23
Aces	3	24
% First serves in	70	56

Match score: McEnroe defeated Sadri 7-6 (5-3), 7-6 (5-3), 5-7, 7-6
(5-3)
Time of match: 4 hours 15 minutes

*From Hensley (1979).

sistency, you can view the data in Table 4-2 which is from the 1977 U.S. Open Singles Final between Jimmy Connors and Guillermo Vilas. As you can see, Connors actually lost the match with his forehand ground stroke while hitting down the line. Therefore, you obviously need to strive for consistency as a key strategy in your game. But you can't sacrifice velocity just to keep the ball in play. Before examining how you can hit with both velocity and control, let's examine the game styles of

TABLE 4-2   Match Statistical Summary
1977 U.S. Open Singles Championship*

J. Connors versus G. Vilas
Forest Hills, N.Y.

	Connors	Vilas
Total errors committed	90	72
Forehand	70	36
Backhand	20	36
Crosscourt	35	33
Straight ahead	55	39
Hit from backcourt	77	56
Hit from midcourt	8	6
Hit from net	5	10
Long	27	27
Wide	19	6
Net	2	5
Long and wide	42	35

Match score: Vilas defeated Connors 2–6, 6–3, 7–6, 6–0

*From Hensley (1979).

several pros. This will show that you can play many different ways and still net excellent results.

VARIOUS GAME STYLES

When Borg was active in tournament competition, he would hit very hard ground strokes that cleared the net by as much as 10 feet. Because of the topspin he used, the ball stayed in play and consistently landed near the baseline. McEnroe, on the other hand, is incredibly effective with his ability to change the speed of his shots, using different spins to disrupt the opponent's timing. In contrast, Jimmy Connors uses two ball speeds: hard and harder. He hits net skimmers that would seem to knock the racquet out of your hand.

All three of these pros use different match strategies because of the way they hit the ball. Borg had what many called an unorthodox swing with a severe rolling of the racquet head in the follow-through. McEnroe, as he hits one of his patented off-speed ground strokes, seems to stand straight up during his swing. Connors looks as though he actually jumps into every ground stroke as he tries to hit the ball as hard as possible. The unique part of each style is that basic laws of physics

(a)   (b)

(c)   (d)

Figure 4–1(a), (b), (c), (d)   Notice how this athlete transfers linear momentum forward by stepping into the shot (parts a and b). The angular momentum is then generated by body rotation (parts c and d).

govern what each player does to the ball. It's these principles of physics that will assist you in learning to hit with control and power.

Generating Momentum

Two very simple concepts affect hitting a ball with control and high velocity. Both involve a transfer of momentum: (1) linear momentum and (2) angular momentum (see Figure 4-1). Linear momentum is derived from the step forward. By stepping into the shot you transfer your body's weight, or linear momentum, forward in a linear fashion to hit the ball effectively.

Angular momentum results from body rotation generated through the legs, hips, and trunk. This may be one of the least-used concepts in tennis because some teachers de-emphasize the effect of body rotation on stroke production. Its lack of use may not be purposeful, however, because so few people understand how angular momentum works, let alone how it is transferred from one body part to another until finally transmitted to the racquet. Simply put, body rotation must occur during almost all tennis strokes with perhaps the exception of the very short strokes; volley, half-volley, and drop volley. To see how you should generate linear and angular momentum, let's examine the body's power supply, starting first with the backswing of a stroke.

The Body's Sources of Power

The Backswing

One of the biggest controversies among tennis players and their coaches is which backswing—straight back, small loop, or large loop—provides the best racquet velocity and control. The traditional train of thought was that a straight-back preparation (seen in Figure 4-2) allowed the most control while the large loop, demonstrated by Chip Hooper in Figure 4-3, allowed the highest racquet velocity. Sport scientists now tell us that it's true that high racquet velocity is generated by the large-loop backswing, but control can be a real problem with that backswing because of the timing necessary to hit a ball effectively. It was found that the small-loop backswing in Figure 4-4 not only allowed for

Figure 4-2 This athlete demonstrates a straight-back preparation.

Figure 4-3   Touring professional, Chip Hooper, demonstrates what a large-loop backswing would look like.

an excellent combination of velocity and control but, just as importantly, helped the body maintain its rhythm during stroking movements. This helped stabilize the athlete's timing in hitting a ball and avoided the timing fluctuations caused by the large-loop backswing. In establishing a stroking rhythm, the small-loop preparation also facilitates the generation of linear and angular momentum.

Linear and Angular Momentum

As mentioned previously, the body utilizes linear and angular momentum to effectively hit a tennis ball. However, neither should work alone! These two sources of power should act together in a coordinated

Figure 4-4   This player illustrates what a small-loop backswing should resemble.

manner. I've already discussed how the transfer of linear and angular momentum is accomplished: by stepping into the shot and rotating the upper body, respectively. The upper body rotation is similar for both a closed- and open-stance stroke. However, since the body rotation is more pronounced for an open-stance stroke, it will serve as a good example of how the transfer of angular momentum occurs.

In the previous chapter, an explanation was given on the footwork involved in effectively hitting a stroke with an open stance. Obviously, there is little transfer of linear momentum into the stroke since the motion of the foot closest to the ball is either directly to the side or slightly behind the impact point. There's a specific reason for the side step, however. As you can see in Figure 4-5, the side step allows the hips and trunk to rotate backward during the backswing. Just prior to the forward swing, there will be a slight push off by the foot closest to the ball. This force, generated from the ground through the leg, follows a specific course of action as depicted by Figure 4-6. After traversing through the legs, it is received by the hips which begin accelerating in a rotary fashion. When the hips reach a certain optimal angular velocity (the word optimal is used here instead of maximal because tennis usually doesn't require maximum force), the trunk begins rotating. This chain of segmental links continues. As the trunk reaches its optimal angular velocity, the upper limb begins to move about the shoulder. The sum of all these integrated forces then results in optimal acceleration of the racquet. When coordinated correctly, this transfer of angular momentum is the factor that can make an open-stance ground stroke so effective.

(a) (b)

Figure 4–5(a), (b) This individual demonstrates how the unit turn is employed in his efficient open-stance forehand drive.

STROKE SEQUENCE:

GROUND REACTION FORCE

↓

LEGS

↓

HIPS

↓

TRUNK

↓

UPPER LIMB

↓

RACQUET

Figure 4-6 This is the sequence of events that occurs as force is transferred through the human body.

Jimmy Connors can serve as an excellent example of someone who uses little linear momentum but who maximizes his angular momentum. The mechanics of Connors' forehand can be viewed in Figure 4-7. You can easily see how the body's rotation brings the racquet head toward impact so well. However, notice when Jimmy leaves the ground during his forehand. In his famous jumping forehand he doesn't leave the ground until just before impact. Therefore, when you see Connors a foot and a half off the ground during his strokes, you should remember that he doesn't leave the ground until the last instant. If Connors jumped any

(a)   (b)

Figure 4-7(a), (b) Notice how Jimmy Connors utilizes no step forward in this forehand drive but how he maximizes his body rotation.

sooner than that, he would lose a great deal of the angular momentum he had generated. In other words, if he left the ground before all the generated force had gotten to his smaller body parts (the forearm and hand), Newton's Third Law (action-reaction) dictates that his larger body parts would react and not send the force forward to the upper limb. Thus, the key to Connors' great open-stance forehand is timing.

Although the open-stance ground stroke can be utilized to hit very effective shots it isn't that easy to perform, which is why the traditional step into the ball is more often recommended. This seems reasonable because this conventional approach permits players to have better control over their bodies, thus usually allowing the stroke to be more efficient. However, it still necessitates synchronizing linear and angular momentum. The timing of the step forward and its coordination with the system of chain links is significant. Many books say to step forward into the shot and swing. It's not that easy!

As the player in Figure 4-8 faces the net and readies to swing forward for a forehand drive, the foot opposite the forehand side of the body will step across and forward in a normal stride-like fashion. The foot will be placed directly toward the point of ball contact or directly forward toward the net. While the opposite foot is striding forward, there is an obvious push off from the hind foot to initiate weight transfer. Once the front foot is planted and is supporting a large proportion of body weight, the transfer of linear momentum is complete. At this point, the force generated from the push off has reached the hips, which begin rotating. This is the important transition: the initiation of

(a)   (b)

Figure 4-8(a), (b) Here you can see a closed-stance forehand. Notice that foot placement is positioned forward and *slightly* to the side.

(a)   (b)   (c)

Figure 4-9(a), (b), (c) This athlete demonstrates the rhythmic "step—then swing" movements involved in a stroke.

angular momentum, through hip rotation, from the linear push off of the hind leg. The trunk will begin its involvement by rotating very soon after the hip rotation has begun. The upper arm will then quickly bring the racquet forward toward impact.

Therefore, the transition between linear momentum and angular momentum is crucial. A mistake in timing could severely hamper stroke production. To help my students understand this timing, I offer a simple phrase for them to think about when practicing. As you see the player doing in Figure 4-9, they are told to "step—then swing," attempting to make their stroke as rhythmic as possible. The rhythm, once learned, will allow the student to graduate to more advanced strokes (e.g., hitting a high ground stroke with topspin). This same rhythmic swing enables players to hit incredibly hard shots with seemingly effortless movement and thus to hit what's known as a solid ball.

THE SOLID (OR HEAVY) BALL

I'll never forget the first time I hit against Tim Gullikson (1983 Wimbledon doubles finalist). I was really pumped up by getting to work out with such a great player. The shots I hit were the best I could muster, but there was one problem that quickly became apparent. Here I was, hitting my best shots and Tim was returning every ball harder than I had hit the previous stroke. Oddly enough, he didn't seem to swing the racquet very fast at all, but he still hit an incredibly solid ball.

The solid, or heavy, ball is a widely misunderstood concept which is most often used at the advanced levels of tennis. Two types of tennis shots exist that are classified as solid balls. These shots are: (1) a stroke like the one hit in the above example; one with a great deal of velocity that feels like it will knock the racquet out of your hand, and (2) a hard ground stroke hit with extreme topspin that seems to take away control of your own shot. Well, how do players develop these awesome strokes?

Hitting a solid ball is one of the key elements in developing offensive ground strokes and service returns. The implications of this are extremely important. By learning to hit a solid ball, you can develop an aggressive, attacking game without having to depend exclusively on the serve-and-volley style of play.

The ability to hit a solid ball depends on how well you can execute the following six steps:

1. Contacting the ball in the hitting zone of the racquet face;
2. Using a firm grip to enhance control and to help with transferring force to the ball;
3. Meeting the ball with the wrist (or wrists, if hitting a two-handed shot) and elbow(s) firm;
4. Imparting the proper amount of spin on the ball;
5. Hitting the ball with a complete follow-through;
6. Contacting the ball at the optimum height for your body size.

Contacting the Ball in the Hitting Zone of the Racquet Face

It's very interesting to me how many people use the term sweet spot to describe where they feel the ball should be correctly hit on the racquet face. Technically speaking, the sweet spot is the center of percussion of the racquet and is usually located somewhere between the center of the strings and the throat of the racquet itself. Contrary to what many believe, the sweet spot is a very tiny point on the racquet face. It's virtually impossible to hit a ball with the sweet spot all the time. However, there is a small area surrounding the sweet spot that permits a player to hit effectively (Figure 4-10). It seems more appropriate to speak of contacting a ball in the hitting zone of the racquet face. The hitting zone is an area ranging anywhere from 2 in. to 4 in. wide (depending on the size of the racquet head) surrounding the sweet spot. Contacting the ball in the hitting zone results in little racquet head rotation and enhances the control of your shot.

It's difficult to practice contacting the ball in the hitting zone of the racquet. When you are swinging your racquet forward toward the ball, it's almost impossible to gauge exactly where impact will occur. Even the pros can occasionally be seen hitting a ball off the frame of their racquet.

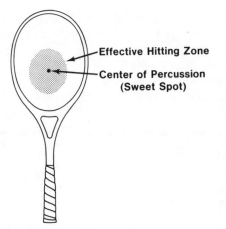

Figure 4-10 The darkened area on the racquet face indicates the size of the racquet's hitting zone.

If you feel a lot of racquet rotation in your hand at ball contact, there are two things you can work on. First, try slowing down your forward swing and simply concentrate on making a firm impact with the ball. Although you have no control over the velocity of the oncoming ball, you can improve your accuracy by slowing the racquet speed. The second thing you can work on is your grip firmness.

Using a Firm Grip to Enhance Control and Transfer Force to the Ball

Numerous biomechanical and tennis authorities (Broer & Zernicke, 1979; Bunn, 1960; Hatze, 1976; Plagenhoef, 1970; Tilmanis, 1975) believe that grip firmness is an important, sometimes the most important, factor in hitting a tennis ball well. By maintaining a firm grip, the player reduces racquet recoil and thereby increases the force applied to the ball. However, a controversy has recently erupted concerning the degree of grip firmness a player should maintain during a stroke. The cause of this debate stems from the research on grip firmness conducted in the late 1970s. Several scientists studied the rebound of a tennis ball as it was fired against the center of a racquet under two conditions: (1) with the racquet firmly clamped in a vise grip as in Figure 4-11, and (2) with the racquet standing balanced on its butt end. In other words, they simulated two extremes of grip firmness: a very strong grip and no grip at all. Amazingly enough, the ball rebounded with similar velocities in both cases. They concluded that there is no time for the racquet to move appreciably while impact occurs, so the effect of a free-standing racquet on ball speed equaled that of a clamped racquet. This implies that grip firmness may not be that important. Bear in mind, however, that these

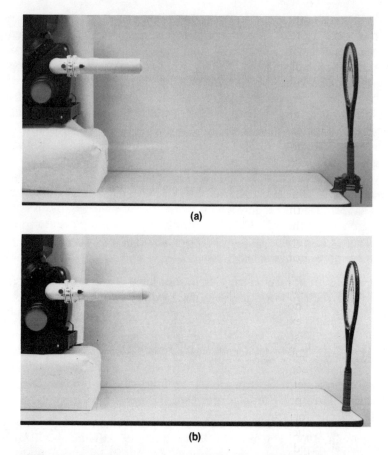

(a)

(b)

Figure 4–11(a), (b)   These pictures depict a laboratory simulation of the firmest grip possible (the clamped racquet in part a) and the loosest grip possible (the free-standing racquet in part b).

studies were concerned with central impacts on a motionless racquet and it's already known that a large majority of impacts are off-center.

My colleagues and I conducted an experiment to see what the effects of grip firmness were for off-center ball contacts. Balls were impacted against a racquet when it was free to rotate and when it was firmly clamped at the handle. It was found that ball rebound velocities were slightly (although not significantly) higher in the clamped situation for respective off-center contacts. The important observation, however, was that in the clamped condition each ball rebounded directly out from the racquet face. For the free-to-rotate condition, the ball left the racquet at an errant angle. Therefore, it seemed that regardless of the effect of grip firmness on rebound velocity, the lack of a firm grip will cause poor ball control.

Bruce Elliott (1982) has done some of the more contemporary work in this area. Instead of using motionless racquets, he constructed a mechanical arm with a hand grasp that would hold the racquet at varying tensions. As a ball was fired from a ball machine, the racquet arm was triggered and swung forward with a velocity comparable to that of a skilled male player. He found a 7% reduction in rebound velocities from the firm to light grip. Elliott concluded that a firm grip was absolutely necessary to increase the power of a stroke and to improve control.

Since we know that a firm grip is required in tennis, let's discuss what it is that makes a firm grip. If you simply hold the racquet in front of you, the grip used is probably very light; just tight enough to support the racquet. If you swung at a ball with this grip, two things would probably happen: (1) the racquet would fly out of your hand as it was swung forward and (2) the muscles of your forearm would not be set to control the racquet during impact and you'd lose control of the shot. When preparing to hit a shot, a light grip can be maintained during the backswing but, as you swing the racquet forward, the grip should be squeezed firmly to enhance your stroke. The grip need not be a death grip, but it should be firm enough to minimize racquet rotation at impact.

We should examine the reasons why a firm grip is necessary to play skilled tennis. First, we know a firm grip is required to generate sufficient power and control at impact. However, there's more to it than that. As you swing the racquet forward, a centrifugal force is created which tries to pull the racquet out of your hand. Your grip during the swing must be tight enough to prevent this from happening and to orient the racquet head correctly for impact.

For a racquet to have sufficient impetus when hitting a shot, force must be generated from other body parts. The transfer of force through these body segments culminates with the hand giving impetus to the racquet. Therefore, a firm grip is of utmost importance as it serves as the final link in this transfer of momentum.

There is a point of no return as far as grip firmness goes, however. Newton's Third Law says that "for every action, there's an equal and opposite reaction." The tighter you squeeze the racquet, the more force that's transmitted to your hand and forearm, especially from those off-center impacts. It will take practice to determine how firm your grip should be. As a test, if the racquet turns in your hand or if you are having difficulty with control, your grip may be too loose. If you experience a great deal of vibration or force into your hand, forearm or elbow, loosen your grip a bit and refer back to the section in Chapter 2 on grip selection to be sure you're using the correct size.

In summary, it seems to me that the controversy concerning grip firmness should be put to rest. When awaiting the opponent's shot, a loose grip should be used. However, a firm grip must be recommended at impact for several reasons: (1) to maintain control over the racquet head as it readies to hit the ball, (2) to provide optimal racquet velocity as it's swung forward, (3) to impart ample force to the ball at impact, (4) to prevent the racquet from twisting in your hand during ball contact, and (5) to effectively link the force generated by the body's kinetic chain to the racquet.

Meeting the Ball with the Wrist(s) and Elbow(s) Completely Firm

Keeping the wrist(s) firm when meeting the ball is another integral part of hitting a solid ball, as is keeping the elbow(s) firm. For example, Kathy Jordan utilizes heavy underspin on most of her backhand drives, but notice in Figure 4-12 how firm the elbow and wrist are held at impact. As force is transferred through the body's kinetic chain, it must pass from the trunk to the upper limb. The three joints in the upper limb (shoulder, elbow, and wrist) are integral in insuring that optimal force reaches the racquet. When a player attempts to hit a solid ball, there should be no excessive wrist or elbow movement regardless of the shot type attempted.

Remember that there are two ways to hit a solid ball: (1) by hitting a high-velocity shot and (2) by hitting a fairly hard shot with heavy topspin or underspin. The above rule applies in both situations. When hitting a hard stroke, the upper limb joints need to maximize the force transfer from the trunk. When you want to hit a solid ball with a great deal of spin, you still should not use excessive joint action.

Although spin production will be discussed in depth in Chapter 6, there are some things you should be aware of relative to this topic. For

Figure 4-12 Notice how firm Kathy Jordan seems to hold her wrist and elbow at the impact point of her one-handed backhand drive. Although some joint action may have occurred prior to impact, an athlete will try to be firm when hitting a penetrating ground stroke.

Figure 4-13   Observe how little upper limb joint action takes place during Bjorn Borg's topspin forehand drive.

example, you can incorporate the wrist and elbow to hit a lot of topspin on the ball but not to hit a high-velocity shot with heavy topspin. Borg can serve as an example of someone who hits fairly hard and with much topspin. Many people think he is a wristy player because of his exaggerated follow-through. However, a high-speed film analysis as seen in Figure 4-13, shows that Borg's elbow and wrist move very little before impact, but move a great deal after the ball has been hit. This allows him to hit a heavy ball with topspin.

The best way for you to work on this part of your game is to practice driving the ball deep into your opponent's court either flat, with topspin, or with underspin. Net clearance will depend on the type of shot. A flat ball with high velocity should not clear the net by more than 5 feet, whereas one with topspin could clear the net by as much as 10 feet. If you have access to a videotape machine, have someone take some pictures of you as you play. Ask them to get views from the side and from behind. This will give you the total picture of what your body parts are doing. Just remember that as you practice, you shouldn't try to hit excessive spin but only enough to provide optimal results.

Imparting the Proper Amount of Spin on the Ball

The correct amount of spin simply means that you impart enough spin on the ball to keep the ball from going out and to keep the opponent on the defensive (refer to Chapter 6). Too much spin takes away from the horizontal velocity of the ball because spin is caused by the vertical motion of the racquet. When the racquet moves vertically to produce spin, you sacrifice forward racquet speed. Figure 4-14 shows the racquet motion when hitting a ball with little topspin. In contrast, Figure 4-15 depicts the racquet motion during a heavy topspin stroke. Figure 4-16 illustrates strokes where the hall is hit with slight underspin and heavy

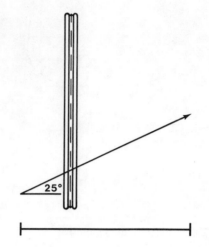

Figure 4-14 This diagram depicts the linear racquet motion when hitting *slight* topspin.

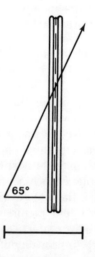

Figure 4-15 Here you can see the linear racquet movement when hitting a heavy topspin ground stroke.

underspin. In all four cases, the racquet travels the same total distance (as denoted by the length of the arrows), but the forward motion is shortened when imparting excessive topspin or underspin. When the forward motion is less and still occurs over the same time period, the ball will not receive as much forward force and will not travel as fast. A common mistake of many advanced players is using excessive spins and still trying to hit the ball very hard. Very few players can hit a lot of spin and consistently maintain control.

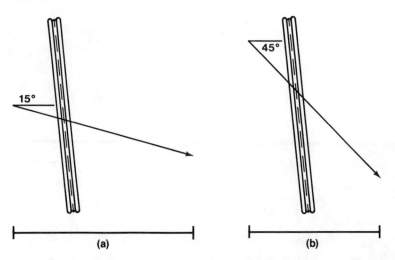

Figure 4-16(a), (b)   These pictures illustrate the racquet movement necessary to hit slight underspin (a) and heavy underspin (b).

You should work on hitting shots that clear the net by 4 to 6 feet and are deep into your opponent's court. By doing this, you'll have to hit penetrating strokes with slight spin. Having depth in the court and clearance above the net as your practice goals, you should see significant improvement in your shots.

Hitting the Ball with a Complete Follow-through

Some of the factors determining how well you hit a solid ball are difficult to monitor (e.g., where the ball hits on the racquet face). However, follow-through may be the most important factor of which you have total control. The only way you can hit penetrating ground strokes is to swing the racquet head through impact effectively. Until the ball has been hit, there can be no racquet head deceleration during the forward swing. Even though the ball has already been hit, you can learn a great deal about your stroke from how you follow-through.

Many players finish their follow-through with the racquet pointing across the net (Figure 4-17). This means that their swings must follow an arc as it travels from the fully-prepared position to the end of the follow-through. Other players wrap the racquet over their shoulders, as you see in Figure 4-18. And still others follow-through with the racquet face directed skyward, as demonstrated in Figure 4-19. There is nothing wrong with any of these follow-throughs, but you must consider one thing as you accelerate the racquet through impact into your follow-through. Don't think of how you will follow-through but of how the racquet face will travel through impact. One cue I give my athletes is to think of making the strings follow the ball as long as possible when it's

Figure 4-17(a), (b)   These athletes show how many tennis players finish their follow-through on the forehand drive.

Figure 4-18(a), (b)   Another type of follow-through involves wrapping the racquet over the shoulders.

hit. That phrase has had pretty good success in swinging through impact with control.

A complete swing with a full follow-through is necessary to achieve maximum velocity while imparting the correct amount of spin on the ball. In order to hit through the ball, you must strive to hit it well in front of your body midline (Figure 4-20). Hitting the ball behind the middle of

Figure 4-19 This athlete demonstrates a follow-through where the racquet faces upward.

the body forces you to swing upward quickly and not hit the ball effectively (Figure 4-21). A forward contact point will allow you to transfer all bodily forces to the upper limb and to attain a high racquet velocity. As you hit the ball, practice a long follow-through after impact. This will help you to continue accelerating the racquet through impact.

Contacting the Ball at the Correct Height for Your Body Size

The final component of hitting a solid ball is meeting the ball at the optimum height for your body. This is a big factor in separating good tournament players from the pros. It is not really that they're lazy, but

(a)   (b)

Figure 4-20(a), (b) Notice where ball contact occurs for these athletes on the forehand drive.

(a)   **(b)**

Figure 4–21(a), (b)   When you are forced to hit the ball behind your body midline, your swing will usually be abrupt with little direct force behind it.

most competitors often let the ball get too low before hitting it, which makes it difficult to hit a penetrating ground stroke. One extra step or step and a half forward and aggressive ground strokes are within reach. Figure 4-22 illustrates three different heights at which a ball may be met.

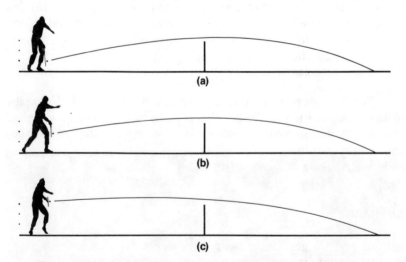

(a)

(b)

(c)

Figure 4–22(a), (b), (c)   These diagrams illustrate how much easier it is for a competitor to hit a penetrating groundstroke when he/she strives for a proper impact point relative to his/her own body. Observe the different points of ball contact (a—near ankle level, b—slightly above knee level, and c—near waist height) and the respective ball flight trajectories from those impact points. Therefore, each athlete should strive to contact a ball near waist height whenever possible.

The top diagram shows a ball that has been hit about 12 in. above the ground (well below knee level for someone 6 feet tall). The ball must follow a fairly steep upward path to clear the net and land deep in the opponent's court. If you wish to swing hard at the ball, you have to impart a great amount of topspin on the ball so that it will be sure to land within the court boundaries. Although heavy topspin is one way of hitting a solid ball, I think you'11 see how much easier it would be if the contact point was a little higher above the ground.

The ball in the middle diagram is met just below net level (2½ feet high). The high-velocity shot must follow a slightly upward path so gravity won't pull the ball into the net. The amount of spin necessary to bring the ball into the court will be less than that required in the top diagram (assuming the two balls are hit at the same velocity). Because the ball in the middle diagram doesn't have to be hit with as much upward trajectory as the one in the top picture the stroke could provide higher ball velocity even though it still might have too much topspin to give the true effect of a solid ball.

The ball in the bottom diagram is at the ideal height for a 6-foot tall person to hit a solid ball: approximately waist height or slightly above. The ball does not have to follow a steep upward path to land with depth in the opponent's backcourt and requires less spin to keep it within the court boundaries. The ball in the bottom diagram can be traveling at a higher rate of speed, making it a more offensive shot. In addition, the racquet head could be accelerated more vertically when the ball is contacted in this position, giving the ball greater topspin if desired.

There is basically one way to position your body so that the ball is contacted at the proper height. As you prepare to hit each stroke, you must move your feet. By quickly moving forward on a short low-bouncing ball or backward on a deep, high-bouncing ball, you'll be amazed at how your strokes will improve. As well as being able to hit a consistently solid ball, your stroke will be moving in a similar pattern each time, making all of your shots more consistent.

SUMMARY

As you practice generating more force behind your shots, always be aware that tennis is basically a control game. Power will do little good if you have no control over your shots. Slowly try to combine the benefits of your body's physical capabilities by utilizing linear and angular momentum in an optimum combination. By using your body parts in synchrony, you will develop a sound power supply. Don't try to hit excessive spins but think of *driving* the ball into your opponent's court. Proper footwork will also help you reach your goal of hitting a solid ball.

By hitting the ball at the desirable height relative to the court and your body, you will be able to optimize your force transfer to the ball.

Therefore, try to pay careful attention to the concepts described in this chapter. If you practice them diligently, you should be able to greatly improve your ground strokes. By learning to hit consistently aggressive ground strokes, you will be capable of playing an offensive, attacking game without having to rely on the serve-and-volley style of play. Due to the tremendous changes that tennis has undergone in the past few years (e.g., slower courts and high performance racquets), the ability to hit offensive ground strokes is quickly becoming the way to develop a winning tennis game. The development of these types of ground strokes combined with shot consistency should be the goal of every tournament tennis player.

REFERENCES AND RECOMMENDED READINGS

Broer, M.R., & Zernicke, R. (1979). *Efficiency of Human Movement*. Philadelphia: W.B. Saunders.

Bunn, J.W. (1960). *Scientific Principles of Coaching*. Englewood Cliffs, N.J.

Elliott, B.C. (1982). Tennis: The influence of grip tightness on reaction impulse and rebound velocity. *Medicine and Science in Sports and Exercise*, (**14**)5, 348-352.

Hatze, H. (1976). Forces and duration of impact and grip tiqhtness during the tennis stroke. *Medicine and Science in Sports and Exercise*, (**8**)2, 88-95.

Hensley, L.D. (1979). Analysis of stroking errors committed in championship tennis competition. In J. Groppel (Ed.), *Proceedings of a National Symposium on the Racquet Sports*. University of Illinois at Urbana-Champaign, Conferences and Institutes, 225-236.

Plagenhoef, S.C. (1970). *Fundamentals of Tennis*. Englewood Cliffs, N.J.

Tilmanis, G. (1975). *Advanced Tennis for Coaches, Teachers and Players*. Philadelphia: Lea & Febiger.

CHAPTER 5

The One- Versus Two-handed Backhand: Which is Better?

How would you react if I told you that a two-handed backhand is easier to hit than a one-handed backhand? What if you read that there is very little difference in reach between one-handed and two-handed backhands? Both of these statements are true, even though many traditionalists might argue vehemently against them. However, their arguments become very outdated when compared to the findings of recent sport science research. Before applying these results to your game, we should discuss how these strokes came into being and how various authorities view them.

The one-handed backhand has been used since tennis began in the 1870s. The two-handed backhand was virtually unheard of until the 1930s when Vivian McGrath became the world's first highly ranked player to compete with it. Very few players used the two-handed backhand after that until the last decade when it became popular with the likes of Bjorn Borg, Chris Evert Lloyd, Jimmy Connors, and Tracy Austin. But why the sudden return of the two hander?

WHAT THE EXPERTS SAY

Authorities offer various reasons for the recent prominence of the two-handed backhand. Some say today's players used it when they were

(a)   **(b)**

Figure 5-1(a), (b) It seems obvious that with two hands on the racquet, as in picture a, the athlete can better control its motion than
when using only one hand (b).

young because they didn't have enough strength or confidence to control
the racquet with a one-handed backhand. In Figure 5-1, you can see an
excellent tennis player who has a good two-handed backhand but can't
hit a one-handed stroke very well. Proponents of the one-handed backhand feel that the two-handed stroke is an affectation and state that the
swinging of a tennis racquet with both hands is unorthodox and cumber-
some. They go on to note that newcomers to the game appear to be
caught in the grip of a revolution because of a desire to imitate the top
players in the world.

Advocates of both types of backhand drives have proposed that
their preferred stroke should be hit similar to a forehand. This immediately raises a great deal of skepticism. In the forehand, for instance,
an eastern, semi-western, or western forehand grip is usually recommended and ball contact should occur over the front foot. To hit a one-
handed backhand effectively, however, a grip change is necessary and
ball contact must occur ahead of the front foot (Figure 5-2). In addition,
a completely different set of muscles is used for racquet control, making
similarity of swing mechanics virtually nonexistent. The forehand and
two-handed backhand are much more similar, as shown in Figure 5-3. To
hit a two-handed backhand, two eastern forehand grips can be used
(although the base hand can be changed to a continental grip if desired)
and ball contact usually occurs over the front foot just as in the forehand. In fact, many say that using a two-handed backhand is just like
hitting a forehand from the opposite side.

Reach

Since both hands are used on the two hander, proponents of the one-
handed backhand have time and time again denounced it for its lack of

Figure 5-2 This player demonstrates where ball contact must occur for an effective one-handed backhand drive.

reach. In a high-speed film study I conducted on 36 highly-skilled players, I could find no difference in reach between the two strokes. See for yourself by comparing the various views of one-handed and two-handed backhands in Figure 5-4. When the players in my study didn't have to run for shot preparation, ball contact for each stroke occurred about the same distance from the body. The immediate reaction to this statement usually stimulates the following question: What about the situation when a player is really stretched out for a backhand return? We can visualize how the pros can lunge at a shot with a one-handed backhand, but what about those players utilizing a two-handed backhand? Could they also reach the wide shot? Probably not! However, how many of those lunging one-handed backhands have you seen hit for winners? Very few, I'm sure. Most of those wide shots are returned as defensive underspin drives or lobs. They are not penetrating, offensive strokes. My

(a)   (b)

Figure 5-3(a), (b) These pictures demonstrate how similar the impact points are for a forehand and two-handed backhand.

Figure 5–4(a), (b), (c), (d) In this series of photographs, compare the distances of impact from the athletes' bodies. You should be aware that the impact point for the one-handed backhand occurs slightly ahead of the front foot while impact for a two-handed backhand occurs nearly even with the front foot.

point is that a player who has an effective two-handed backhand (Figure 5-5) can learn to hit those one-handed lunges and develop a sound defensive underspin drive or lob. Therefore, there is really no rationale for avoiding a two-handed backhand due to a supposed lack of reach, especially on balls you can easily get prepared for.

Low-bouncing Balls

The one shot that a two hander could have problems with is a low ball in front of the body (Figure 5-6). Obviously, with both hands on the racquet the player must get lower to return such a shot offensively. With a one-handed backhand, the body doesn't have to get quite as low to hit

(a)   (b)

Figure 5-5(a), (b)   Although the competitor seen in these figures has an extremely effective two-handed backhand (a), he is quite capable of performing a one-handed lunging maneuver when he is pulled wide of the court.

the ball effectively. Therefore, the player with a two-handed backhand must get to the ball quicker for a higher ball contact point or learn to hit that low shot with one hand as the player in Figure 5-7 is doing.

The Role of Muscular Strength

It's been fairly well accepted that the one-handed backhand requires greater strength on the part of the performer. Since only one upper limb is used to generate force in swinging the racquet, and the arm can't rely on trunk action as much as a two-handed backhand, it makes sense that more strength is demanded by the one-handed stroke. Beginners using a

Figure 5-6   A two-handed backhand often has problems with a low-bouncing ball. The player in this figure has used extremely good footwork to get in position for the return.

Figure 5-7 May Lou Piatek demonstrates how a player who utilizes an effective two-handed backhand can learn to hit a low shot with one hand as you see here.

one-handed backhand are often seen cramping the elbow (holding it very close to the body as in Figure 5-8) for exactly that reason. They don't have the physical capabilities to wield the racquet efficiently. In contrast, the cramping motion is not usually seen in the two-handed backhand because the swinging motion necessitates the elbows being fairly close to the body. In addition, the racquet should actually be less difficult to swing with two hands around the handle than when only one hand is used.

If the individual has difficulty in swinging the racquet with one hand, poor racquet head control can result and cause (1) poor shot place-

Figure 5-8 This player really doesn't have the physical capabilities to support and swing the racquet with a one-handed backhand. Notice how she is swinging by holding the upper arm close to the body indicating she needs to support the racquet motion with her trunk.

(a)   **(b)**

Figure 5-9(a), (b) These figures depict two of the movements players will often go through in trying to hit a backhand drive over the net. Picture (a) shows a player leading with her elbow when preparing to hit the ball while picture (b) shows a player using a great deal of wrist action in trying to make contact with the ball.

ment, (2) difficulty in imparting spin, (3) severe turning of the the racquet head during and after impact, and (4) a late ball contact point. To accommodate these problems, the player may lead with the elbow or drop the racquet head just prior to impact (Figure 5-9) to help propel the ball over the net.

Utilization of the two-handed backhand could eliminate these difficulties (although not always). It's definitely true that with two hands on the racquet handle you can swing upward more effectively and maintain better racquet head control, especially when beginning to hit topspin drives.

Spin Production

Strength also plays a significant role when hitting topspin. As seen in Figure 5-10, topspin is often difficult to hit using a one-handed backhand due to the additional strength needed to swing the racquet at a steep upward angle. In comparison, imparting topspin with a two-handed backhand is comparatively simple. A problem often associated with the two-handed backhand is a player's ineffectiveness at varying spins. Since two hands are used, increasing the upward swing angle to produce topspin can easily be accomplished. However, a problem often exists in maneuvering the racquet in a high-to-low motion for underspin and a side-to-side motion for sidespin. Some two handers will compensate when hitting an underspin shot and follow-through with only one hand to facilitate the high-to-low action. Notice the athlete in Figure 5-11 as she

(a)   **(b)**

Figure 5-10(a), (b), By comparing pictures (a) and (b), one can see how much more difficult it is to swing the racquet with one limb when trying to hit a topspin drive.

hits an underspin shot on the backhand side. Although she follows through with both hands on the racquet, many players will follow through with only one hand on the racquet. A one-handed follow-through might allow a smoother racquet action through impact, facilitating the high-to-low motion for hitting underspin.

High-bouncing Balls

Advocates of both backhands have reported that high-bouncing balls can be hit more effectively with their preferred stroke. This all depends on the physical capability of the player and what type of shot is to be hit. It's

(a)   **(b)**   **(c)**

Figure 5-11(a), (b), (c) This athlete shows how an underspin ground stroke should be hit from the baseline using a two-handed backhand. Notice that the racquet is slightly above the impact point (b) which facilitates the downward action causing the underspin.

Figure 5–12(a), (b), (c)   When hitting a high one-handed backhand, it
is recommended that underspin be used.

extremely difficult to hit a one-handed backhand with topspin on a ball
bouncing at head height. Underspin is usually recommended for this shot
(Figure 5-12), and the ball usually cannot be hit with a very high velocity.
In comparison, a player with a two-handed backhand can hit a ball
around head height aggressively (Figure 5-13) either flat or with topspin
and usually with a higher ball velocity than is possible with one hand.

Disguise

The two-handed backhand has been lauded as being easy to disguise. It's
said that the second hand on the racquet has the ability to maneuver the
racquet head at the last possible instant, directing the ball to a part of the
court unsuspected by the opponent. If you've ever played a tournament

Figure 5–13(a), (b)   With two hands on the racquet, it is possible to
hit a high-bouncing ball with topspin as you see here.

(a)   (b)

Figure 5-14(a), (b) As you would look across the net at a player hitting this shot, it actually seems as though a wrist flick is involved in hitting a short cross court passing shot.

match against someone with a good two-handed backhand (Figure 5-14), it really does seem that they can flick the wrist at the last second to pass you crosscourt when all along you were figuring on a down-the-line shot. However, the same can be said for a player with a good one-handed backhand. The next time you are practicing with someone who has an excellent one-handed backhand, stand at the net and practice a volley-passing shot drill. After you've hit a couple of volleys in the drill, your opponent should try to pass you either down the line or crosscourt. Your job is to read the passing shot before it is hit. If your opponent is skilled

(a)   (b)

Figure 5-15(a), (b) This athlete demonstrates that a similar wrist flick may be seen when hitting a short cross court one-handed backhand.

at this type of drill, I think you'll find out that a good one-handed back-hand can also be well disguised (Figure 5-15).

   With all the previous information in mind, what decisions can we make about the two types of backhand drives? Both strokes have some obvious advantages and disadvantages. We also found out that some of the claims made for or against one of the strokes may be unjustified. This information can help you in determining how your backhand might be enhanced by using one or the other technique, but we can go a step further into our analysis. By studying the two strokes from a sport scientist's viewpoint, I think you'll get the answers to some of your unresolved questions.

WHAT SPORT SCIENCE TELLS US

Do you remember the high-speed film study discussed earlier where the backhand techniques of 36 highly skilled tennis players (18 for each stroke) were analyzed? One significant finding dealt with the number of body parts used in each stroke and how they're properly coordinated. For example, players using each stroke type had a small circular back-swing. This enabled each person to have a slightly higher racquet head speed at impact than with a straightback backswing; thus hitting a high-velocity shot.

   For the one-handed backhand, it was found that five distinct body parts are used prior to impact. After the player in Figure 5-16 steps

(a)   (b)   (c)

Figure 5-16(a), (b), (c)   In this series of pictures you can see how the different body parts are used when hitting a one-handed backhand drive. Notice that there is slight hip and trunk rotation during the swing and that the hip and trunk do not completely open up until the ball has been hit.

toward the ball, the hips turn slightly, transferring their momentum to the trunk which begins rotating. Then the upper arm moves about the shoulder. This upper arm motion is transferred to slight forearm movement which, in turn, causes the hand and racquet to position for ball contact. Ball contact must occur about 12–14 in. ahead of the front foot to insure transfer of momentum along all these body parts and to orient the racquet face vertically with respect to ball flight.

It's because of those five body parts that many people have trouble playing tennis with a one-handed backhand. They really can't coordinate all five segments. How many times have you seen individuals playing who lead with the elbow or drop the racquet head to help hit the ball over the net? What happens is that those players can use the major body parts but, when it comes to transferring the momentum to the forearm through the elbow, they lose the coordinated pattern and lead with the elbow. Some can transfer the momentum through the elbow to the forearm well but can't get it by the wrist efficiently and severely drop the racquet head, causing an awkward follow-through. The two-handed backhand is a different story.

The two-handed stroke only utilizes two body parts to swing the racquet toward impact. After the player in Figure 5-17 begins the forward transfer of linear momentum and steps toward the ball contact point, the hips begin to rotate. They in turn cause the trunk to rotate. The arms of both limbs rotate with the trunk while no movement occurs at the elbows or wrists up to impact. That is, the trunk and arms rotate as one body part. After impact any number of contortions occur for the

(a)   (b)   (c)

Figure 5-17(a), (b), (c) Compare the hip and trunk movement in a two-handed backhand with that of the one-handed backhand seen in Figure 5-16. Observe the amount of hip rotation that has occurred in picture (c) while the shoulders are bringing the arms and racquet toward the impact point.

follow-through depending on each player's idiosyncracies. The most common follow-through is to wrap the arm and racquet over the shoulder.

Our question about a wrist flick in either stroke can now be answered. Slight wrist movement does occur in a skilled one-handed backhand but little is seen in the two-handed backhand. I must add, however, that all the players in my study were hitting down-the-line backhands. You may see more (but not a lot more) wrist motion in both strokes when going crosscourt. My suggestion is to keep the wrist(s) firm in both strokes and forget about flicking the ball crosscourt.

EASE OF SKILL ACQUISITION

Which backhand is easier to learn? It seems that a player might be able to develop the skills to hit an effective two-handed backhand more readily. Intuitively, if you have to learn one of two strokes and you know that all characteristics of each are similar except that one only uses two major

TABLE 5-1

Characteristic	One-handed Backhand	Two-handed Backhand
Number of body parts used	5—hips, trunk, arm, forearm, hand, and racquet	2—hips, trunk and arms
Spin production	Underspin easy; topspin can cause problems	Topspin easy; underspin can cause problems
Disguise	Similar	Similar
Strength	More required because of one-arm involvement	Less required because of two-arm involvement
Grip change	Not absolutely necessary but is recommended	You can select a slight change or no change
Reach	Similar when you get adequately prepared and properly positioned	Similar when you get adequately prepared and properly positioned
Low returns (ankle high)	Easier to retrieve	You usually must use one hand
High-bouncing balls (head high or slightly above)	Easy but usually you must use underspin	Easy to hit flat or with topspin
Vulnerability to injury	With one arm accepting shock, wrist and elbow are susceptible	Elbows and wrists are better protected

body parts and the other uses five, which do you think would be easier to learn?

SUMMARY

I feel that it is important to say that both the one-handed and two-handed backhands have specific characteristics that are conducive to optimal performance. However, as you determine what would be the best for you and your game, consider some of the attributes in Table 5-1. With these concepts in mind, decide what areas give you the most problem when playing. You may even want to write down how the use of either a one- or two-handed backhand would help or hurt your own game. It is really an individual choice.

In my opinion, the two-handed backhand can be an incredibly overpowering stroke. I feel also that it can be learned much easier than its counterpart. Many people have downplayed the two hander because of its lack of reach. However, this criticism seems unjustified. The stroke not only will provide the athlete with a greater ability for hitting topspin and high-bouncing balls but it also allows the player to use more trunk rotation in generating force to hit the ball. In addition, the two-handed stroke allows the shock of impact to be split up and absorbed by two arms instead of one. Many think the two-handed backhand is a fad or a psychological placebo that gives more confidence. I think it can serve as an asset to a player's game and that the stroke is here to stay.

CHAPTER **6**

Ball Spin: Why Use It! When to Use It! How to Use It!

GLOSSARY

Coefficient of Restitution — Describes how a body (e.g., a ball) will deform and regain its original shape during and after impact.

Friction — The opposing forces found between two surfaces (e.g., a racquet and ball, or a ball and the court).

Sidespin — Describes the type of ball spin when the ball rotates sideways (like a top).

Topspin — Describes the type of ball spin when the top of the ball rotates away from you as it travels toward your opponent.

Underspin (or backspin) — Describes the type of ball spin when the top of the ball rotates toward you as it travels toward your opponent.

There is only one way to produce ball spin in tennis. You must accelerate the racquet head through impact to brush the backside of the ball either in an upward direction for topspin or a downward direction for underspin. The more vertical you swing the racquet (in either direction) the more ball spin you'll produce. The angle of the racquet face at impact may have some influence on the amount of spin, but it will primarily determine the direction of ball flight off the racquet.

The amount of spin a player imparts on the ball, combined with a high stroke velocity, often determines how effective the player will be.

For example, Bjorn Borg is the master of topspin. When watching him play on television, you've probably heard the announcers speak of his tremendous looping topspin shots and how difficult it is for the opponent to return any of those shots effectively. In contrast, other players, like Evonne Goolagong who uses a great deal of underspin and Jimmy Connors who employs very little spin, still reign as world-class players. What is it, then, about spin that makes each player's style a winning one?

Spin can be used for various reasons. Some players like to use underspin (or backspin) a lot because they feel they can better control shot placement. Sometimes, however, an underspin shot cannot be hit with great force (as in a passing shot) and still be controlled. Other players, who may attack the ball more aggressively, utilize topspin. They seem to hit balls that would normally fly beyond the baseline but don't because of the imparted topspin. Still other competitors have been observed to use sidespin on some strokes, especially on the serve. Because so many variations of ball spin exist, it behooves anyone wishing to excel in the game to learn about spin and why it's so important in championship tennis.

THE EFFECT OF SPIN ON BALL FLIGHT

As a tennis ball travels toward the opponent its flight is affected by the surrounding air. Air turbulence creates tiny eddies around and behind the ball that cause it to slow down. When the ball is spinning, the air has an even more significant effect on ball flight. If a ball has topspin it is rotating in the direction in which it's traveling, and the spin carries with it a small boundary layer of air (Figure 6-1). On the side where the boundary layer is opposite to the oncoming air, a high-pressure area is built up (Figure 6-2). On the opposite side of the ball the two air flows

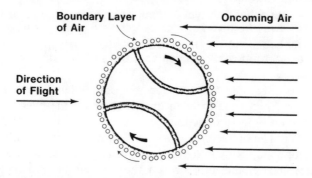

Figure 6-1 As the tennis ball encounters the oncoming air notice how a small boundary layer of air travels around the tennis ball as it spins.

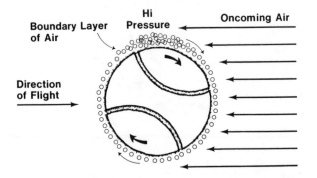

Figure 6-2 In this diagram you can see how the boundary layer of air being carried around the ball in a topspin direction interacts with the oncoming air to create a high pressure zone above the ball.

are in the same direction and the velocity of the oncoming air is slightly increased, causing a low-pressure area. The ball tends to move toward the side where the least pressure exists. With topspin, pressure is greater on top of the ball and reduced under the ball, forcing it to drop more rapidly than normal. That's why a heavy topspin shot has such a looping trajectory. With underspin (Figure 6-3) the opposite occurs: Greater pressure is underneath the ball, keeping it in the air longer.

Just as ground strokes are most often hit with either underspin or topspin, the majority of serves are hit with varying types of sidespin. As seen in Figure 6-4, the rotation on a served ball ranges (for right-handed players) from a 3 o'clock type sidespin on the ball to an almost 12 o'clock topspin. In flight, the ball with sidespin acts the same as a baseball pitcher's curve ball. It travels in a curved path opposite the side of the

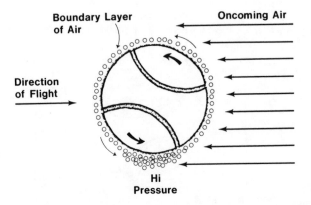

Figure 6-3 When the ball has underspin, the boundary layer travels around the ball in the direction of the underspin creating a violent interaction beneath the ball. This interaction creates a high pressure zone under the ball.

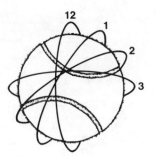

Figure 6-4   This figure depicts the types of ball spin that can usually be imparted. Note that a 12 o'clock spin is topspin while a 3 o'clock spin is sidespin.

ball where the high-pressure zone is created (Figure 6-5). In fact, if a right-handed player imparts an extreme amount of sidespin (3 o'clock spin), the ball might deviate several feet to the left of the path it would have taken if no spin were hit.

In summary, consider a hypothetical situation (Figure 6-6) where three ground strokes are hit with an identical velocity and trajectory, but with different types of spin. Let's assume a ball hit with no spin will land halfway between the service line and baseline. Relatively speaking, a ball with topspin will land near the service line, and a shot with underspin will bounce near the baseline.

THE EFFECT OF SPIN ON BALL BOUNCE

Spin also affects how the ball bounces. Do you remember from high school physics that if you look into a mirror at an oblique angle you see

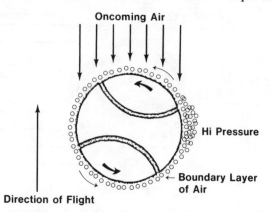

Figure 6-5   When a ball has been hit with sidespin, this view from above shows how the high pressure zone is created where the turbulence occurs between the boundary layer of air and the oncoming air.

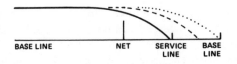

BASE LINE   NET   SERVICE   BASE
                                LINE   LINE

Figure 6-6 If three balls are hit from the same height at the same velocity with the same angle of departure from the racquet, you can see how their flight patterns might differ from this picture. If a ball with no spin (--) lands halfway between the service line and baseline, a ball with topspin (—) would bounce shorter into the opponent's court while a ball with underspin (...) would land further into the opponent's court.

something across the room that's situated at the same angle to the mirror as you? Similarly, if two people stand equidistant and at the same angle from a mirror and both look toward the mirror's center, they will see each other. In theory, a tennis ball will bounce in the same manner if it has no spin. That is, the angle of the bounce from the court surface will be similar to the angle of approach to the tennis court. Due to frictional factors and the coefficient of restitution between the ball and tennis court, however, the angle of rebound is almost always greater than the approach angle.

Spin causes the ball to bounce much differently. For instance the rotation on a ball with topspin pushes backward against the court, causing the ball to rebound at a lower angle than a ball with no spin (Figure 6-7). That may be hard for you to believe, especially considering that all of Borg's opponents hit their returns of his topspin shots about head high every time. It's true that Borg's shots often bounce higher than one would normally expect, which has in the past been attributed to the immense amount of topspin on the ball. To explain this phenomenon, two things are important. First, you must remember that topspin makes the ball bounce at a lower angle than a ball with no spin only when the angles of approach to the surface are identical. Second, a topspin drive causes

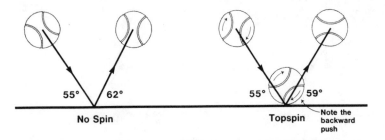

55°   62°   55°   59°

No Spin   Topspin   Note the
                                         backward
                                         push

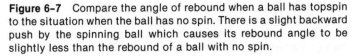

Figure 6-7 Compare the angle of rebound when a ball has topspin to the situation when the ball has no spin. There is a slight backward push by the spinning ball which causes its rebound angle to be slightly less than the rebound of a ball with no spin.

the ball to loop over the net and this looping effect forces the ball to strike the surface at a much steeper angle than would a ball without spin. Therefore, the reason for Borg's high-bouncing topspin forehand lies in the ball's sharp approach angle to the court. If a spinless ball were to bounce on the court at the same angle of approach and with the same velocity as one with topspin, the spinless ball would bounce at a greater angle to the court surface.

The bounce of a ball hit with underspin is different from that of a ball hit with topspin. Whereas a topspin shot causes the ball to bounce at a lower angle than a ball with no spin, the rotation on the ball with underspin causes it to bounce at a greater angle under certain conditions. When the ball approaches the court at 45° or greater, the underspin causes the ball to push forward during contact with the court, which forces the ball to slow down and rebound more vertically than normal. Figure 6-8 illustrates the different bounces caused by no spin and underspin. Though the two balls approach the surface at the same angle, the one with underspin tends to *grab* the court and bounce at a steeper angle. A variety of circumstances can also cause a tennis ball to bounce differently. For instance, the slower the court surface, the greater the effect of the spin on the bounce. On clay or Har-Tru (an artificial clay surface), the ball with underspin, for example, will tend to stop and sit up. On grass it will skid and rebound very low and fast.

The angle at which the underspin shot hits the court surface will also affect the rebound. High-speed film analyses demonstrate that a soft, lazy ground stroke hit with underspin will cause the shot to sit up and give the opponent a chance for an easy return. A sliced drive that just clears the net will usually skid and take a low bounce, forcing the opponent to bend his or her knees to hit the return. This difference in rebound is caused by the angle of approach to the surface (Figure 6-9). In general, where the angle is greater than 45°, the ball with underspin will bounce more vertically. When the ball hits the court at less than 45°, it

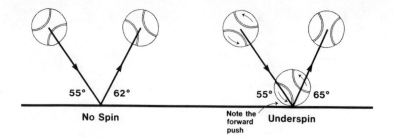

Figure 6-8 Notice the effect that underspin can have on the rebound of a tennis ball. There is a slight forward push by the spinning ball against the court which causes its rebound angle to be slightly greater than if the ball had been hit with no spin.

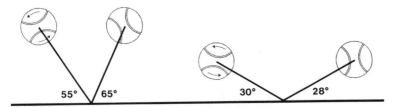

Figure 6-9   Observe how the rebound of a ball with underspin can be effected by its approach angle to the tennis court. As a rule of thumb, if the ball with underspin approaches the court at greater than 45° the result is a greater rebound angle. However, when the ball with underspin approaches the tennis court at an angle less than 45° the rebound is occasionally less than the approach angle.

will usually skid and stay very low. Therefore, the intent of most underspin ground strokes is to drive the ball deep into the opponent's court with a low trajectory, forcing the opponent to hit up for net clearance. When John McEnroe, for example, decides to go to the net on a short shot that bounces below net level, he'll seldom use a topspin approach shot. As the player in the adjacent pictures approaches the net (Figure 6-10) he chips the ball (puts underspin on it) as low over the net as possible, but will send it very deep. When this shot is hit with a low trajectory, its approach angle to the court will be low causing it to skid and remain low after the bounce. This forces the opponent to hit upward on the ball so it will clear the net, thus bettering your chances for a put-away volley. If, however, the chip shot goes too high over the net, the approach angle to the court will be too steep and the ball will take a high bounce, giving the opponent a chance at an easy winner. It's therefore imperative not to hit an underspin ground stroke too high over the net.

(a)   (b)

Figure 6-10(a), (b)   Notice how this athlete swings in a high-to-low fashion to hit the ball with underspin as he approaches the net.

When the ball with sidespin bounces the ball can take several paths, depending on the type of ball spin. The ball hit with a 3 o'clock or 2 o'clock spin will tend to continue in its original curved path once it bounces. That is, the spin actually has little effect on the bounce in terms of changing the ball's velocity or height of bounce. Now, a ball with a 1 o'clock spin (somewhat of a combination of topspin and sidespin) will tend to bounce in a direction opposite to that of ball flight (depending on the court surface). The slower the court (i.e., clay), the more effect the spin will have, causing the ball to bounce in the opposite direction to ball flight. On a fast court surface (i.e., grass), however, the spin's effect will be lessened and the ball's bounce won't be as severe. If the bounce can cause the ball to deviate extremely from its flight path, this serve type can be very effective, especially as a second serve.

APPLICATION OF SPIN

Since ball spin can be used to vary the pace of a rally or keep the opponent from getting grooved to one type of ball bounce, it must become an integral part of any player's repertoire. The problem now is how to apply spin.

For example, there used to be three common trains of thought regarding the application of topspin: (1) swinging upward with a vertical racquet face to brush the backside of the ball, keeping the wrist and elbow fairly firm (Figure 6-11); (2) swinging the racquet similarly, but

Figure 6-11 In this schematic of Ivan Lendl drawn from films taken at 100 frames per second, it should be noted that topspin can be hit by swinging in a low-to-high fashion while employing little wrist or elbow movement.

Figure 6-12   Brian Gottfried demonstrates how the elbow and wrist joints can be used to achieve greater vertical acceleration of the racquet.

employing movement at the elbow and wrist which accelerates the racquet head more vertically (Figure 6-12); and (3) rotating the hand and forearm at contact, trying to roll the racquet face over the ball (Figure 6-13). Since many coaches have contradictory theories about topspin, I decided to investigate the two major elements of spin production: (1) the linear motion of racquet in imparting spin and (2) the angular motion of the racquet prior to contact, at contact, and after contact. A high-speed camera shooting pictures at 500 frames per second was used to film 30 skilled players as they hit flat shots (with no spin), shots with topspin, and underspin shots.

(a)   (b)

Figure 6-13(a), (b)   This player attempts to roll the racquet over the ball. Due to the time period of impact, rolling the racquet face over the ball is virtually impossible.

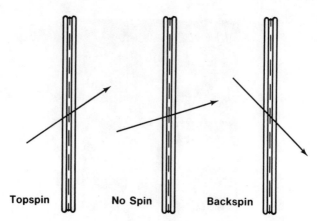

Figure 6-14 Notice how the linear motion of the racquet heads differ for hitting various ball spins. The angle of racquet head motion when hitting topspin is almost twice as steep as that for hitting no spin. The angle of the racquet head movement when hitting backspin (underspin) is in a steep downward direction.

Although it is extremely difficult to hit a ball completely without spin, the players all swung slightly upward (Figure 6-14) when attempting to hit a flat ball. The reasons for this are two-fold: (1) the swing must be directed upward to have the ball clear the net (if a completely horizontal swing were used, the ball would never make it over) and (2) to hit a spinless shot, the forward spin of the approaching ball must be negated which can be accomplished by an upward swing.

When comparing the two lines for no spin and topspin in Figure 6-14, you can see that the swings of these players became almost twice as steep when hitting topspin. This tells us that the linear motion of the racquet head is important in spin production. In addition, two other points should be discussed. First, the more vertically the athlete accelerated the racquet, the more spin was produced. Second, in contradiction to one of the previously mentioned theories on topspin production, none of the players rotated the racquet head, in their attempts to put additional spin on the ball. Following impact, however, racquet head rotation was seen in many of the strokes. One reason for this rotation could be off-center ball contact on the racquet face, which was seen in about 95% of the impacts. When a ball hits below or above the center of the racquet, as shown in Figure 6-15, torque is created, forcing the racquet head to rotate.

Another reason for racquet head rotation is that as the arm and hand cross the body (Figure 6-16), they naturally rotate so the palm of the hand faces down. Place a racquet in the hand and the racquet rolls over with the hand. This action is caused by the structure of the shoulder and does not occur until the arm crosses the body, obviously well after a tennis ball would have been hit.

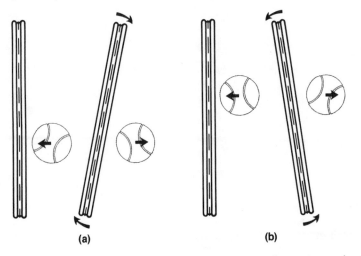

(a)   (b)

Figure 6-15(a), (b) From this diagram one can see how a torque is created from off-center impacts below the central axis of the racquet (a) and above the central axis of the racquet (b).

Regardless of the reason for its occurrence, no racquet head rotation contributed to ball spin and by the time any turning did occur the ball was clearly off the racquet and on its way back over the net. Therefore, the rotation of the racquet face couldn't possibly have affected the amount of spin on the ball. The racquet face at impact was usually very

(a)   (b)

Figure 6-16(a), (b) Observe how the rolling over of the hand, forearm and racquet occurs as the upper limb crosses the chest. This movement involves forearm pronation and shoulder rotation which takes place due to the structure of that joint.

Figure 6-17 Notice the low-to-high motion and vertical racquet face utilized in Bob Lutz's topspin backhand.

close to being vertical (Figure 6-17). This tells us that the angle of the racquet face plays only a minor role in imparting topspin, which may cause some skepticism, as we've all seen professional players apply topspin by seeming to roll over the ball. But the facts remain; it just doesn't happen.

Hitting Topspin

If rolling the racquet face is not the way to produce topspin, how is it done? Let's assume that you are standing at the baseline in your ready position with the racquet held with the opposite hand at the throat. As soon as you see the ball come off the opponent's racquet traveling toward your forehand side, employ the unit turn and help take the racquet back with the opposite hand (Figure 6-18). Just prior to initiating the forward swing, step toward the ball (or use an open stance if you prefer) and then swing upward to establish contact just in front of the body. The follow-through should end above the head. At first, you should keep your wrist and elbow firm when hitting topspin. Once the precise timing is developed, you can try to gain additional spin by employing various wrist and elbow movements to accelerate the racquet head more vertically.

In which case (topspin or underspin) do you think more rotation can be put on the ball? This question may sound a little ridiculous, but it actually plays a big role in controlling a tennis shot. To give you a clue to the answer, what type of spin do most players resort to when the pressure in a match gets tight? Although not everyone does it, many competitors (especially the nervous ones) use underspin in these situations and they don't even know why. To help you understand the reason, think how a ball is rotating following its bounce from the court. Ninety-nine and nine-tenths percent of the time it will have topspin on it (Figure 6-19).

(a)   (b)

Figure 6-18(a), (b) Notice how this tennis player hits a forehand drive with topspin. In picture a the racquet is quickly getting to a position below the impact point and will strike the ball in an upward fashion leading to the high follow-through seen in picture b.

However, imagine that you have just hit that ball and it's spinning the same way as it heads toward your opponent. Now the topspin, as you viewed it before you hit the ball, is underspin. Therefore, when you hit a topspin return, you must stop the spin already on the ball from the bounce and change it so the ball rotates in the opposite direction. When underspin is placed on the ball you merely add to what's already there.

Hitting Underspin

To hit a ball with underspin, the backside of the ball must be struck in a downward fashion (Figure 6-20). Past coaching has offered several

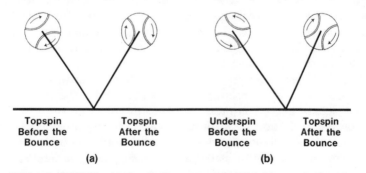

| Topspin Before the Bounce | Topspin After the Bounce | Underspin Before the Bounce | Topspin After the Bounce |

(a)   (b)

Figure 6-19(a), (b) Notice in these two conditions how a ball, with initial topspin (a) or underspin (b), has topspin on it following the rebound.

(a)   (b)   (c)

Figure 6–20(a), (b), (c) The author demonstrates how to effectively hit an underspin drive. Notice that the racquet action must be high-to-low and that the racquet face should be *slightly* bevelled at impact.

methods of hitting underspin correspondingly similar to those suggested for topspin; the most ludicrous being to turn the racquet under the ball at impact. Our study of the 30 highly-skilled players clearly indicated that underspin can be imparted only by brushing the backside of the ball in a downward manner with the racquet face slightly open as you see in Figure 6-20. Now, it's true that whenever the pros hit an underspin backhand, their racquet seems to turn under the ball at contact and continue to turn after the ball leaves the racquet. Remember that the time of ball contact is so short that it's impossible to rotate the racquet head fast enough to aid in spin production. One reason the racquet may turn is that it's natural in the follow-through position for the hand and forearm to turn so the palm faces downward (the same thing happened when hitting a lot of topspin). Another reason for the turning effect may be the force produced by the ball on the racquet face. In almost all of the 30 cases studied the ball contacted the racquet in the hitting zone slightly above the center, causing the racquet to rotate as shown in Figure 6-15(b). To hit an underspin shot, you must take the racquet back higher than you would for a routine ground stroke. With the racquet head turned slightly open, you must swing downward to hit the ball. Don't chop at the ball, but *drive* slightly downward through impact. The racquet head should continue its downward path until after ball contact. At this point, the pros will usually move the racquet up around shoulder height. This is a rhythmic motion that isn't really necessary for everyone. The downward swing, however, is essential to hit underspin. The open racquet face simply combines with the downward swing to send the ball over the net. Just be careful not to open the racquet face too much, causing the underspin shot to have a high trajectory and allowing the ball to sit up for the opponent. Kept low and deep, underspin becomes a useful weapon.

A mastery of spin production is a necessity to play championship tennis. To prevent your opponent from getting grooved to your strokes, you must be able to vary ball spins. In doing so, you can keep the opponent off-balance and also prevent him or her from easily setting up to tee off on your shots. Remember, however, that your opponent will also try to do the same thing. Therefore, the mastery of spin not only includes the ability to hit various spins but also to read the trajectory of the opponent's shot and prepare according to how it will bounce toward you.

Making a Good Volley Even Better

GLOSSARY

Bevelled (open) Racquet Face — When the racquet face is slanted backward away from the vertical.

Closed Racquet Face — When the racquet face is slanted forward past the vertical.

Continental Grip — The grip that situates the V of the swinging hand over the inside bevel of the racquet handle.

Dishing — Trying to move the racquet under and around the ball during a volley.

Drive Volley — A shot that is hit before the ball bounces by using a long stroke.

Eastern Backhand Grip — The grip that situates the base knuckle of the swinging hand over the top flattened surface on the handle as the racquet face is oriented vertically.

Eastern Forehand Grip — The grip that situates the V of the swinging hand over the top flattened surface on the handle as the racquet face is oriented vertically.

Ground Strokes — Shots that are hit following the bounce of the ball.

Half-Volley — A stroke that contacts the ball immediately after it bounces off the court surface.

Punch Volley — A shot that is hit before the ball bounces by using a very short stroke.

All skilled tennis players know how to volley; probably because very little racquet movement is required, making it a fairly simple shot to hit. However, many volleys lack the velocity, depth, and penetration necessary to play championship tennis. Some tennis players may not realize the difference in a punch volley versus a drive volley, how crucial the timing is on the split-step prior to volleying, or what the trajectory of the ball off the racquet should be. This chapter will address these topics and more. But perhaps we should first discuss two major causes of poor volleys: (1) an emphasis on developing ground strokes while learning to play and (2) a fear of being at the net.

Many world-class players, such as Guillermo Vilas, Jose Luis-Clerc, Chris Evert Lloyd (Figure 7-1), and Andrea Jaeger, are re-knowned for their effective ground strokes and not so much for their volleys. Although all of these athletes have excellent volleys, you seldom see them at the net because their strength lies in their ground strokes. Since they don't practice volleying as much as someone like Navratilova or McEnroe, their timing at the net isn't as good as it could be. Realizing this, some tennis players tend to lose confidence in their volley during important points. When Andrea Jaeger beat Chris Evert Lloyd in the finals of the 1982 Avon Championships of Oakland, she was asked what her basic strategy was. Her reply was, "I wanted to be patient and wait for her to make a mistake. I really didn't want to go to the net or do something else that was stupid." Jaeger showed a great deal of respect for Evert Lloyd's ground strokes and she knew her own ground strokes were her strongest attributes. However, a person with an aggressive approach shot and volley may have been able to end the points a bit easier; thus, the need to develop all aspects of your game.

Another cause of problematic volleys is fear. This is understandable if you imagine yourself in a baseline rally. As you and your opponent hit the ball from baseline to baseline (Figure 7-2), the ball travels at

| (a) | (b) |

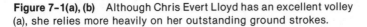

Figure 7-1(a), (b)   Although Chris Evert Lloyd has an excellent volley (a), she relies more heavily on her outstanding ground strokes.

Figure 7-2   Notice how this player has ample time to prepare for the opponent's shot when each player is at his respective baseline.

least 78 ft. You have time to read the opponent's shot, decide what you intend to do with the ball, move into position, and hit the proper stroke following the bounce. Suddenly you realize the opponent has hit a short ball inside the service line and you hit an approach shot, hoping to gain a more strategic position at the net. As the opponent hits the return of your approach shot, the ball will travel only about 50 ft toward you (Figure 7-3) and you need to hit a volley. It's not as easy to follow the ball's trajectory and your timing must change drastically from a routine ground

Figure 7-3   Notice how a player's timing must change when he goes to the net. Instead of being approximately 80 feet away from his opponent when at the baseline, he is approximately 50 feet from his opponent and must react much more quickly.

stroke to the quick reaction and movement of volleying. With all these sudden changes in timing and preparation, it should become obvious why some people fear the net position and how difficult it is for them to volley well during a point.

FOOTWORK IS CRUCIAL ON THE VOLLEY

As with other strokes in tennis, a good volley begins with proper footwork. If you're not in position to hit an offensive volley, you'll have to settle for a more defensive shot to keep the ball in play. This gives your opponent one more chance to hit a winner. So let's talk about proper footwork for the volley.

There are two ways to get to the net: (1) serve and volley and (2) hit an approach shot and advance toward the net. Whichever method is employed, the same footwork must be used as the volleying position is neared. This is the split-step, a step which resembles a movement in hopscotch. We've all seen the pros perform it. For example, once John McEnroe hits a serve in doubles (Figure 7-4), he follows it in and, as the

(a)   (b)

(c)   (d)

Figure 7-4(a), (b), (c), (d)   John McEnroe has an excellent serve and volley maneuver. Notice the split-step occurring just prior to the volley in picture (d).

opponent begins his forward swing, McEnroe spreads his legs slightly (but keeps them parallel with the shoulders) to land in somewhat of a ready position awaiting the opponent's return. This may be the single most overlooked part of volleying.

First, what is the purpose of the split-step? Is it to become stable in a ready position so you can move with equal quickness in all directions? That's partially the answer, but there's much more to hitting a great volley. It's true that, as a skilled tennis player split-steps, we see the feet go apart, but this position should not be static once the landing has occurred. The feet do not simply go apart, land, and stay in that location until the swing is initiated. When the feet separate to split-step, they should seem to generate an elastic quality and bounce out of the split-step and into the volley. If no bounce occurs, the ankles and knees will become major shock absorbers and flex significantly. This forces the player to sink deeper into a crouch position and causes quick reactions to be difficult.

Timing now becomes crucial. Players going into the split-step too soon cannot bounce out of it as quickly because they would be ready for the volley too early for an effective momentum transfer. Players initiating the split-step too late look as though they are running through the volley, causing poor body balance and extremely poor shot control. As a rule of thumb, you should split-step as the opponent begins the forward swing (Figures 7-5). Although not a scientifically valid way of determining when to split-step, this is a good practice since it usually will allow the volleyer to split-step and hit a well-timed volley.

Mechanics of the Split-Step

As mentioned previously, the function of the split-step is to widen the stance, creating a very stable, yet not fixed, base of support upon land-

Figure 7-5   From this rear view you can see how and when the split-step should occur.

Figure 7-6 This player shows how to move forward when hitting a strong volley.

ing. The wider and more stable the base is (within reason), the faster you become unstable toward the direction of the unit turn movement. This allows very fast movements in any direction. The main point, then, is to properly time the split-step action and create a slight imbalance forward in the direction of the volley.

As you prepare to bounce out of the split-step to hit the volley, always try to step forward into the shot as you see the athlete doing in Figure 7-6. When you go to the net, think of your parallel foot positioning in the split-step as being the base of a triangle (Figure 7-7). As the ball approaches, step to the top of the triangle just before making contact with the ball. This will insure a sound transfer of momentum into the stroke. Obviously, there will be times when this footwork will be impossible,

(a)   (b)

Figure 7-7(a), (b) Notice how the feet in picture (a) form the base of a triangle and how the player maneuvers toward the top of the triangle in picture (b).

Figure 7-8 Brian Gottfried demonstrates the upper limb, trunk, and hip movement necessary when hitting an effective volley.

such as when you get jammed by an opponent's stroke or when you must stretch to volley the return. However, by understanding and using this forward weight transfer your volley should improve immensely.

UPPER-BODY MECHANICS IN VOLLEYING

Once the correct lower body movements are accomplished, the upper body comes into play. Assuming that the footwork was precisely performed, as Brian Gottfried demonstrates in Figure 7-8, the hips and trunk should be turned slightly to accommodate a good volleying action. From this point, some tennis players make a serious mistake when volleying. They try to overpower the volley by using a full swing that severely hampers control.

Since hitting the volley with precision is obviously important, it seems necessary to discuss the advantages and disadvantages of two distinctly different volley types: the punch volley and the drive volley. The punch volley, shown in Figure 7-9, refers to a short, compact volley that utilizes very little backswing or follow-through. The drive volley, seen in Figure 7-10, gets its name from an emphasized backswing and follow-through employed by players as they drive the ball into the opponent's court. As indicated earlier, timing is crucial when volleying and this is particularly true with the drive volley. The punch volley must also be a well timed stroke but, because of the longer upper-limb movements required by the drive volley, timing is even more critical. To prove this fact and show how different skill levels are affected by these techniques, my colleagues and I conducted a study on the drive volley techniques of advanced, intermediate, and beginning players. All players were asked to stand in a specific spot on the court near the net and to hit a drive volley directly back toward a target close to the baseline. They were filmed at 200 frames per second as they tried to hit drive volleys toward the target.

Figure 7-9(a), (b), (c)   This athlete shows the proper execution for a punch volley. Note the slight backswing and short stroking maneuver when contacting the ball.

As expected, the skilled players executed excellent drive volleys, hitting each ball near the racquet face center. The intermediate players hit only mediocre drive volleys and most impacts were off-center, causing a great deal of racquet rotation. The beginners, needless to say, had their difficulties. Very few of their drive volleys even made it over the net and all impacts were severely off-center. Only one person hit the target and, interestingly enough, it wasn't one of the advanced players. It was one of the beginners who, after becoming frustrated with drive volleys, used a punch volley. His first and only punch volley hit the target. Further investigation revealed that all the players had more control using a punch volley. Therefore, this study seems important in two respects: (1) that only skilled players have the timing required to hit an effective drive volley, and even their control was suspect when using it and (2) the

Figure 7-10(a), (b)   This competitor demonstrates a drive volley. Compare the difference in the backswing and follow-through with the punch volley seen previously.

punch volley may provide a player with a good deal more control than
the drive volley.

Arm Movement in Effective Volleying

Regardless of whether a drive or punch volley is used, the arm motion of
some tennis players can still cause some serious accuracy problems. As
the players bounce into and out of the split-step, the elbows are often
held close to the body, as you see demonstrated in Figure 7-11. This can
slow down a player's racquet work tremendously. In fact, I'm sure
you've heard how some players are said to have quick hands at the net
because they react to high-velocity shots so well. The hands may have
something to do with it, but the real key lies in the upper-limb positioning. When the elbows are held in tight to the body, the upper limb must
rotate as shown in Figure 7-11. The racquet actually goes into a slight
backswing position that, for many players, can cause late ball contact
and poor control. If the elbows are held slightly away from the body, as
shown in Figure 7-12, the upper limb can be used a bit more effectively
and less rotation at the shoulder will occur. This means the racquet will
not go into a backswing position but will be kept in front of the body as
you see in Figure 7-12. This allows for more effective impact and enables
the player to have quicker hands than if the elbows are held in.

A time when quick hands will be necessary is when reacting to a ball
that hits the net tape. When this occurs the ball usually stays on the opponent's side of the court and you win the point. At times, however, the
ball will hit the net tape and continue toward you in one of two ways: (1)

(a)   (b)

Figure 7-11(a), (b)   The author demonstrates an incorrect elbow
position when preparing to volley (a). When the elbows are held too
close to the body as shown here, notice the contortions he must go
through to achieve a proper racquet position (b).

(a)   **(b)**

Figure 7-12(a), (b) When the elbows are positioned slightly away from the body (a) as you prepare to volley, it will be easier for the racquet to go forward quicker and achieve a proper volleying position (b).

it will hit the tape solidly and barely fall over into your court or (2) it will tip the net tape and skip slightly upward, losing little velocity. When you hear the ball hit the tape, you must react quickly to either: (1) lift the racquet head slightly so if the ball skips up off the net you will have a chance at contacting it, or (2) immediately sprint forward so you can hit the ball before it bounces twice. Although the occurrence of these two phenomena doesn't happen often in a tennis match, I've seen a lot of points won by a player merely reacting to one of the above situations. Remember, your opponent isn't intentionally trying to hit the net tape, so whenever the ball hits the net and comes into your court, your opponent is usually caught off guard and must react with you.

What Grip to Use When Volleying

Since we've studied the importance of proper footwork and body mechanics in hitting volleys, the next step is to analyze how the racquet should be held. This may seem trivial to some players, but how the racquet is oriented in the hand will have a huge effect on how well the ball will be hit and where it will go once hit. Two trains of thought exist when prescribing the grips to be used when volleying: (1) to change grips from an eastern forehand grip for a forehand volley to an eastern backhand grip for a backhand volley and (2) to use a continental grip for volleys on both sides. The primary goal of each technique is to provide the player with a comfortable grip that provides a nearly flat racquet face at impact. There are biomechanical advantages and disadvantages related to either gripping technique, and for quite some time there has been debate over which grip provides the greatest advantages for volleying.

Tennis authorities over the years have been split, not only between which gripping method is best for the beginning player, but also between which technique seems most appropriate as skill rises. Three major schools of thought exist: (1) those instructors who feel that if the continental grip is learned in the early stages of playing and used throughout a career there will be a better chance for advanced stroke development, (2) the teachers who feel the eastern grip change is best taught to beginners and that this technique should be used for the duration of the players' careers, and (3) those experts who are of the opinion that the eastern grip method is best used to teach the novice player but that the player should change to the continental grip as skill develops. This diversity of opinion has made the decision of which method to use a difficult one for any player. Therefore, we need to examine specifically what the experts say about the use of each grip. Then we can apply sports science concepts to the controversy to help you make certain decisions about what might be best for you.

Those who support the continental grip (Figure 7-13) point to several advantages of this technique. The most popular claim is the time factor involved when compared with the eastern grip change. Since the time for stroke preparation is reduced by being at the net, they feel that the continental grip requires less time to execute an effective volley. This group also cites that the player using a continental grip need only be concerned about one gripping method, which would seem desirable in pressure situations. Another claim favoring use of the continental grip is that it provides for a greater degree of adaptability on the part of the player. This technique naturally permits an open racquet face that assists in handling low balls. It is felt that the open racquet face is most adaptable for the various reaction-type situations that occur in net play. Still others claim that the players' comfort and confidence level is improved by using

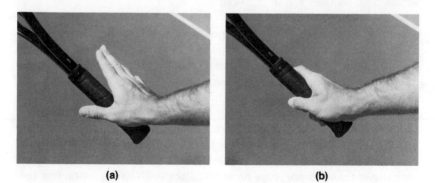

(a)   **(b)**

Figure 7-13(a), (b)   Notice how the V of the hand is located over the inside bevelled (angled) edge of the racquet handle when using a continental grip.

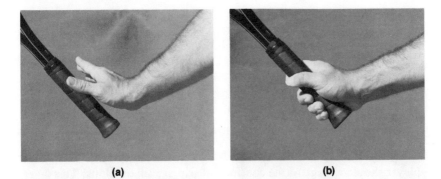

(a)   (b)

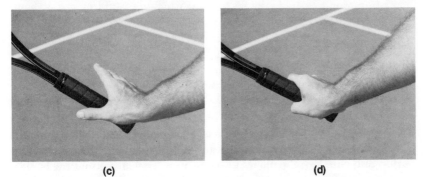

(c)   (d)

Figure 7-14(a), (b), (c), (d)   These are the eastern forehand grip (a and b) and eastern backhand grip (c and d), respectively. Note the positioning of the V of the hand for each grip. In the eastern forehand grip the V is located on the top flattened part of the racquet handle as the racquet face is held vertical. The base knuckle of the forefinger is located on that same top flattened surface for the eastern backhand grip.

the continental grip (since no grip change is required), thus improving their play at the net.

The second school of thought regarding the volley grip includes those coaches who support the notion that the eastern grip-change method is best for the advanced player. Most of these authorities feel there is plenty of time, even in the quickest of net volley exchanges, to make the grip change from forehand (Figures 7-14a and b) to backhand (Figures 7-14c and d). They note that if the grip change is the first move on the player's part, time does not become a factor. These individuals have cited many mechanical advantages corresponding to the eastern grips that make them seem to be the superior choice. They feel that there is increased control on high volleys, better directional control down the line, and greater strength available (due to how the hand is oriented on the handle) for the volley.

(a)   **(b)**

Figure 7-15(a), (b)   Kathy Jordan uses a western forehand grip for *both* the forehand and backhand volleys. Although this grip may be limiting to most players, Kathy is an excellent volleyer.

Still other tennis experts suggest teaching beginners and advanced beginners the eastern grip-change method, but having the students switch to the continental grip as their skill improves. They agree that the beginning player must first learn to develop a vertical racquet face at impact but, as advancements are made in skill, the student should modify their hand position on the racquet to the continental grip. By doing so, the better player can take advantage of the slightly open-faced racquet and time-saving characteristics. It is felt by some veteran tennis instructors that there is time for a pivot and grip change at the beginner's level of play but, as play becomes quicker with increased skill level (see Figure 7-15), there is a need to use the no-change advantage of the continental grip. Some authorities even point out that there may be plenty of time for a grip change at the elite level of competition but that problems often arise due to the difficulty in locating the proper hand position for the eastern grip change. One problem that arises, however, is that the student becomes so comfortable with the grip he or she first uses that the habit is difficult to change later.

Much of the previous information has been derived through the personal experiences and observations of individuals who play and/or teach professionally. Their ideas are sound, but we might be able to go a step further by applying sport science concepts to the problems involved. Therefore, let's analyze what goes into the grip of a mechanically efficient volley.

WHAT SPORT SCIENCE TELLS US ABOUT THE VOLLEY GRIP

The most important aspect of a volley grip is that it orients the racquet face correctly so that an optimum shot can be hit. On high volleys it is necessary to have a near vertical racquet face, but on low volleys the racquet face must be slightly bevelled to help clear the net and place the ball deep in the opponent's court. One difference between the continental grip and the eastern grip is how the racquet face is naturally oriented to the ball at impact. The eastern grip allows the wrist to be in a mechanically sound conformation and easily presents a vertical racquet face to the ball at impact. This allows for a direct force transfer from racquet to ball and ensures a firm, high-velocity shot if desired. Contrary to this, the continental grip normally causes some wrist deviation if used properly and also causes the racquet face to be slightly bevelled backward (as shown in Figure 7-16) so it is open to the ball at impact. This assists the player in putting underspin on the ball because in order to maintain control of the shot while hitting with an open-faced racquet, the stroking motion will be slightly high to low. Interestingly enough, it can be argued that both grip techniques enhance volley control; the eastern grip because it provides optimal ball–racquet impact, and the continental grip because it allows for underspin to be used readily and helps with shot depth due to the open face.

Figure 7-16 Observe how the continental grip causes a naturally open racquet face.

Figure 7-17 This athlete shows how the eastern forehand grip allows a down-the-line volley to be hit with ease. Notice how her upper limb does not suffer through any contortions in moving toward the volley.

One of the most often mentioned disadvantages of the continental grip is the difficulty a player has in volleying down the line on the forehand side while at a position near the center service line. This inside out shot has been a topic of concern. If you use an eastern forehand grip (Figure 7-17), it is fairly easy to go down the line without any significant wrist or elbow contortions. If a continental grip is used, the wrist and elbow must be maneuvered into the proper positions or the player must utilize the unit turn and orient the body so the upper limb won't have to go through these motions (Figure 7-18).

Another mechanical advantage favoring the eastern grip change is on the backhand volley. As you can see in Figure 7-19 an eastern backhand grip allows the wrist to be in an efficient position. In contrast, a backhand volley with a continental grip places a great deal of muscular stress on the forearm (Figure 7-20). From a sports medicine point of view, this evidence alone would favor using the eastern grip change, but it should be pointed out here that very few tennis players actually use a true continental grip for both the forehand and backhand volley.

Although most pros using the continental grip feel they do not change grips between these two volleys, there is evidence suggesting that some form of grip change almost always occurs. As a player prepares for a backhand volley, the thumb and forefinger will remain in place on the racquet handle but there is a slight shift of the heel and hand toward the inside (Figure 7-21). If you have problems understanding why this slight hand shift occurs, try hitting both forehand and backhand volleys with a true continental grip. If sufficient strength isn't present in the wrist extensors (on the back of the forearm), you will most likely experience a great deal of stress in the forearm during the backhand volley. Using the

(a) (b)

Figure 7-18(a), (b) The author demonstrates two maneuvers that usually occur when an athlete using a continental grip wants to volley down the line. Notice in picture (a) how the wrist is severely laid back and the shoulders turned to position the racquet head properly. In picture (b) the trunk must be further deviated to the side while the feet position the body to allow the racquet face to direct the ball down the line.

hand shift, the angle of pull of these muscles is reduced so that the stress isn't as great.

Figure 7-19 Notice how there is an efficient conformation between the hand and forearm at the wrist when using an eastern backhand grip.

Figure 7-20   Notice the potential stress placed on the back of the forearm when volleying with a continental grip.

If you question the time limitations of the slight hand shift in the continental grip, be aware that ample time does exist. The required movement is so small relative to the eastern grip changes that the continental grip hand shift can be made without the use of the opposite hand, whereas an eastern grip change almost always requires use of the opposite hand.

Based on the information available, I would recommend that you use a continental grip on your forehand volley with the slight hand shift being employed to hit a backhand volley. In almost all tennis situations, ample time exists for the hand shift to occur. In addition, it seems that the advantages of having a slightly open racquet face outweigh the ad-

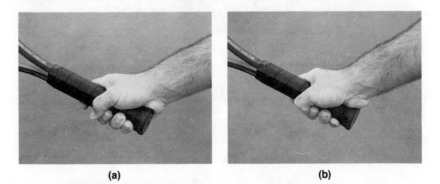

(a)   (b)

Figure 7-21(a), (b)   Observe how the heel of the hand shifts toward the inside when hitting a backhand volley with a continental grip.

vantages of using a vertical racquet face. As for control, both may be good but I feel the high to low racquet action with the slightly open racquet face necessitated by the continental grip allows for better placement and depth of volleys.

MORE ON VOLLEY CONTROL

The discussion of control in volleying leads to four final points that will be listed here and then examined in depth later. First, be sure the racquet face stays firm through impact, and avoid dishing it in an attempt to increase ball underspin. Second, when hitting low volleys try to position your eyes as near the height of impact as is physically possible. Third, never hit down on a high volley unless you are attempting to hit a short volley. Finally, avoid hitting low volleys whenever you can.

Dishing the ball is a phenomenon tried by many players when volleying, sometimes even without the player's awareness. In an attempt to place additional underspin on the ball, the players use not only a slight high-to-low motion but also a dishing action that seems to roll the racquet under and around the ball (Figure 7-22). From the chapter on spin production you should remember that the time limitations of impact won't allow you to dish the ball. A high-speed film analysis of highly skilled players shows that when they dish the racquet, the dishing doesn't occur until after the ball has been hit. A more in-depth examination reveals that there is no racquet head rotation prior to ball contact and that the dishing effect seen is usually a reaction to the impact, not a purposeful movement. Therefore, hit your volleys with a firm racquet. It's all right to let it dish once the ball's been hit, but use no racquet rotation before contact—even on balls below the net tape.

(a)   (b)

Figure 7-22(a), (b)   The author demonstrates the dishing action of the racquet head often seen during volleying.

Low volleys seem to cause a lot of headaches. Regardless of whether the low volley is hit long, into the net, or simply not well enough to suit you, one simple mechanical principle might help: It's fairly well accepted that you will be a more accurate player when your eyes are located near the point of contact. Obviously, some volleys are so low that it's impossible to get your head down that far. A good cue to use would be to bend your knees to situate your seat as low as possible and get your eyes near the level of the volley. Tim Mayotte accomplishes this quite well, as you can see in Figure 7-23. Hitting low volleys like this will increase your accuracy and allow you to be a more offensive player at the net.

Some players feel that an offensive volley should be hit hard and short into the opponent's court. Although these shots are sometimes effective, the volleys are usually so short in the opponent's court that any advantage gained by going to the net is lost because the opponent has so much time to read the volley, judge its bounce, and hit the passing shot. The problem may stem from the fact that the players stand higher than the net and can see more of the opponent's court, which causes them to have an unrealistic sense of depth perception. Therefore, they feel that they must hit downward on each volley. This usually finds the volley in the net or so short in the court that it has little effect. These players don't realize that gravity can be of great assistance in tennis and thus they don't let it work for them. I think all of us will agree that the deeper a volley is in the court the more effective it becomes (unless you want to hit short angles, of course). This means that you cannot hit the ball downward; you must direct it at least straight out from the racquet face or even slightly upward. To get the feeling of how deep volleys should be hit, try volleying the ball long at first and slowly try to bring the subsequent volley back into the court. Don't be concerned with velocity until

Figure 7-23 As Tim Mayotte demonstrates, it is important to get your body down on low volleys so your eyes are as near the level of impact as possible.

you obtain good control. Once you develop a deep, controlled volley, you'll be amazed at how much more effective your net play will be.

Another facet of volleying that separates good volleyers from great volleyers is where the ball is contacted relative to the player's body. Many players, even though they may have excellent volleys, never perform to their potential at the net because they're lazy. These athletes will go to the net and hit a ball wherever it happens to be relative to their own bodies. In other words, they don't close in toward the net and attack the volley. A great player will always close in on an opponent's shot, attempting to volley it before it drops below net height. By doing this they become more effective from two standpoints: (1) they are closer to the net, thus minimizing the possibility of volleying the ball into the net and (2) they hit the ball at a higher point than they would if they waited for it to reach them in a position further from the net. Both situations allow the volleyer to be a more offensive player. Therefore, be watchful for an opponent's lob and, whenever possible, don't let an opponent's shot dip below the net and force you into a more defensive position.

THE DROP VOLLEY

One of the most overused shots in tennis is the drop volley. It's a great shot to have in your repertoire, but many players use it too often. The purpose behind a good drop volley is to catch the opponent off guard when he or she is expecting a hard drive or to hit a winner when the opponent is pulled out of position. However, it is also a crowd pleaser. When hit properly, it comes across as a beautifully contrived work of art, receives many oohs and ahs from the crowd, and generally reinforces a tennis player's actions when at the net. The problem is that whenever a player hears the crowd's reaction to a beautiful drop volley, the player seems to do it again and again. After a while the opponent is actually waiting for the player to hit another drop volley so he or she can pounce on it.

Since most players tend to utilize the drop volley too much, I have developed a philosophy that I use often. To those players I say, "Don't hit a drop volley unless your opponent has fallen down and has one foot caught under the back fence." This usually makes my point that the drop shot should not be overused. However, when executed at the proper time, the drop volley can be a devastating weapon.

To hit an effective drop volley, you merely need to decelerate the racquet head at impact. Remember that on a punch volley or a drive volley you are trying to sharply strike the ball and accelerate the racquet head through impact. During the drop volley you must slow down the racquet head as contact with the ball occurs. Players have different ways of doing this. Some say to soften the grip while others say to drop the racquet quickly as the ball contacts the racquet head. I'm not sure I agree with either of these philosophies. Your goal must be to slow down the racquet head as you approach impact. However, softening the grip or dropping the racquet head at the last second may not really do that. One cue that might help you is to try to just *touch* the ball. As a goal, practice hitting your drop volley and making the ball bounce five times before it gets to the opponent's service line. In addition, don't hit the ball with a trajectory too high over the net. Remember that the higher the ball goes over the net, the more time the opponent has to react and run down your drop volley. You must strive for low net clearance and several bounces prior to reaching the opponent's service line.

In summary, remember that the drop volley should only be hit in specific situations. If the opponent is not out of position or if you have not caught your opponent off guard, any psychological momentum you

(a)   (b)

(c)   (d)

Figure 7-24(a), (b), (c), (d) In picture a, you can see how John McEnroe uses a quick pick-up maneuver when half-volleying. In pictures b, c, and d the athlete demonstrates how a proper half-volley should be performed. Notice how he meets the ball just as it rebounds from the court to guide it over the net.

gain from trying to hit the drop volley will be lost. Instead, the opponent will gain a great deal of psychological momentum in retrieving a shot that you thought was going to be a clean winner. Therefore, be smart, and learn to hit the drop volley in the proper manner and at the right time.

THE HALF-VOLLEY

Sometimes you can't avoid hitting a low shot when you are at the net. Bearing in mind that you should try to volley the ball whenever you can, there will be situations when the ball will bounce first and you will have to hit what is known as a half-volley. This short pick up stroke can be extremely effective, but the timing and mechanics are often very difficult. A player hitting a half-volley must use a very short backswing and contact the ball as it rises from the court (Figure 7-24). The ball should be guided to the desired position in the opponent's court, usually short or deep and down the line.

Don't panic if you must hit a half-volley. Think of it as a control shot. Used effectively, it can keep the opponent off balance and be an excellent weapon in your stroke repertoire.

SUMMARY

In summarizing what's been said about the volley, I think it's important that you analyze everything relative to your own net play. Does the grip you use, combined with your volley mechanics and footwork, allow you to hit deep, short, and angled shots with control? You may also want to consider how balanced you are when approaching the net and during the split-step. Be sure you transfer your body momentum forward in the correct manner and that it's appropriately timed with your volley. Don't try to overpower the volley. Use the velocity of the opponent's shot to your advantage and avoid extraneous racquet head movement before ball contact. For high volleys, hit the ball straight out from the racquet face unless you want to hit a short volley. For low volleys, get your seat and eyes low, near the level of impact. By employing these characteristics in your net game, your volley should become a very penetrating weapon.

CHAPTER 8

The Serve and Overhead: Your Ultimate Weapons

GLOSSARY

Extension — Usually refers to the increasing of the angle between two body parts (e.g., straightening the knee from a flexed position).

External Rotation — Refers to the position of the swinging shoulder in the serve and overhead when the upper limb is in a position of elbow flexion and the hand is located behind the head during the backswing.

Flexion — Usually refers to the decreasing of the angle between two body parts (e.g., knee bend or elbow bend).

Ground-Reaction Force — The force emitted by the ground on the body as the athlete pushes off.

Hyperextension — When the hand bends backward at the wrist.

Internal Rotation — Refers to the shoulder in the serve and overhead when the shoulder rotates to move the hand and racquet forward toward impact.

Pronation — Rotating the hand from a palm-up position to a palm-down position.

Serving a tennis ball and hitting an overhead smash are similar to pitching a baseball. When good leg action is synchronized with the proper upper body mechanics, these strokes can be devastating weapons.

Many athletes, however, have trouble with them because they either don't use the entire body to their advantage or they have poor timing between the various body segments. This creates even more problems for the player wishing to play championship tennis because the serve and overhead are possibly the most important strokes in the game.

The serve starts every point in a game and can be very effective in helping you win a point, or it can be a backbreaker in a match if it is not hit well. In other words, it can cause you to win or lose. The same can be said for the overhead smash. If you are in position for an overhead you have an edge over the opponent and should be able to attack with the smash. On the other hand, if your overhead technique is poor and you can't hit the ball effectively, the opponent ends up with the psychological momentum and can take the offensive. Therefore, it seems necessary that we discuss the mechanical aspects of a skilled serve and overhead in terms of the force that must be generated and how that force is transferred through the body to the racquet and ball.

DEVELOPING FORCE FOR THE SERVE AND OVERHEAD

Contrary to what many believe, the force provided by the body to hit an effective serve or overhead isn't developed at the trunk and upper limb. The majority of force is generated from the ground in the form of a ground-reaction force. Remember Newton's Third Law: For every action, there is an equal and opposite reaction. When serving or hitting an overhead, the feet push against the ground and the ground pushes back with the same amount of force. In Figure 8-1, notice how Stan Smith flexes and extends his knees to create a solid ground-reaction force. Few tennis players use this principle to its fullest advantage. Obviously the one thing that would increase the ground-reaction force would be the correct use of knee flexion and extension. Two problems often prevent players from correctly using the knees: (1) too little or too much knee flexion and (2) improper timing of the knee movement relative to the rest of the stroke.

The proper amount of knee flexion actually is dependent on an individual's strength and coordination. Consider this example: If you were trying to jump as high as possible vertically, would you bend your knees just a little or would you go into a deep crouch? I doubt if you would do either. There is an optimum amount of knee flexion unique to each individual. Without enough knee bend poor ground-reaction force will be generated, while too much knee flexion will result in excessive body motion and an inefficient transfer of force from the ground.

The second problem encountered by many tennis players is poor timing of the knee action relative to the entire serving or overhead mo-

(a)   (b)

(c)   (d)

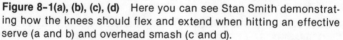

Figure 8-1(a), (b), (c), (d) Here you can see Stan Smith demonstrating how the knees should flex and extend when hitting an effective serve (a and b) and overhead smash (c and d).

tion. Remember that the segments of the body act as a system of chain links whereby the force generated by one link, or body part, is transferred in succession to the next link. When the transfer of that force is not efficient, the outcome of the stroke will be less than desirable. Since the knee bend is among the first of all body movements involved in the serve and overhead smash, it functions as the foundation for other segmental actions.

Figure 8-2   Notice how the knees are flexed as the ball toss is completed.

One instructional cue I use with the players I coach is telling them to flex the knees as the ball is tossed on the serve (Figure 8-2). As the athlete prepares to swing forward (as in Figure 8-3) he or she is instructed to *thrust and throw*. The thrusting action, about to be initiated by Mark

(a)   (b)

Figure 8-3(a), (b)   Here you can see how the knees extend and initiate a throwing type action as the forward swing is completed.

(a)   **(b)**

Figure 8-4(a), (b)   As Mark Dickson (a) and Tim Gullikson (b) show, the thrusting action is gained from knee flexion and its subsequent forceful extension.

Dickson and Tim Gullikson in Figure 8-4, gets them to flex and then extend the legs forcefully toward the impact point while the throwing action, which Stan Smith prepares to use in Figure 8-5, initiates the proper body rotation. The same concept can be used when hitting an overhead (Figure 8-6). Thus the force in serving and smashing is generated through a ground-reaction force caused by knee flexion and extension. Once the knees extend, the sequencing of body parts begins with the first segment—the hips.

Figure 8-5   The throwing action is gained from hip and trunk rotation.

(a)   (b)   (c)

Figure 8-6(a), (b), (c)   The same concept of thrusting and throwing can be used when hitting an overhead smash.

Hip Action

Until recently, many teachers have questioned the involvement of the hips in hitting a serve or overhead and have therefore tended to overlook their importance. Teaching pros have, in the past, been aware of the legs and trunk because those segmental movements are obvious. However, contemporary knowledge now dictates that hip rotation may be the most crucial component in making the difference between a great serve or overhead and a mediocre one. This is the area of the body where a skilled player transfers the linear and angular momentum generated by the legs to the trunk. If the hips are omitted from the movement, the serve won't be very effective. This is why Roscoe Tanner has such a great serve. Many think he hits the ball while the toss is rising and, because of his quick motion to do so, he generates a high racquet velocity. First of all, he doesn't hit the ball on its way up. The ball is usually at the peak of the toss and is motionless when Tanner makes contact. This means that his reaction to the toss is not the reason for his high racquet velocity. Tanner produces his racquet speed by the way he uses his legs and rotates his hips and trunk. Without the phenomenal timing of his hip rotation, even Roscoe Tanner's serve might be only average instead of one of the world's best.

Trunk Rotation

Once the force is transferred effectively to the hips and they reach their maximum rotation velocity, the trunk is rotated. The amount of trunk rotation varies from player to player. Some players can generate a great deal of angular velocity from very little trunk rotation, but most good servers and smashers have a large amount of trunk ro-

(a)   (b)

(c)   (d)

Figure 8-7(a), (b), (c), (d) In this series of photographs the service motion of John McEnroe can be viewed. Observe the high amount of body rotation he employs to hit his powerful serve.

tation. As McEnroe hits his serve, for example, the hips can be seen facing to the side and slightly behind the court (Figure 8-7). In coiling the body this way, an athlete is able to create a great deal of angular momentum with the trunk. However, it is extremely difficult to employ this excessive trunk rotation efficiently and still be able to sequence the rest of the motion properly. If you're not used to it, you might hurt your back. It's important to be aware that trunk rotation is a necessary link in the chain, but don't try to overpower the serve with a lot of trunk movement. Work into it naturally so that you can slowly develop an efficient force transfer from the trunk to the upper limb.

(a)   (b)

Figure 8-8(a), (b)   Notice the movement about the shoulder as Stan Smith swings forward toward ball contact in the serve (a) and overhead smash (b).

Upper Limb Motion

The next component in the system is rotation of the arm about the shoulder. In Figure 8-8, Stan Smith demonstrates some of the shoulder actions seen in serving and hitting a smash. By the time the trunk reaches its peak rotation velocity, the swinging arm should have gone through all of its preliminary actions and should be ready for the forward swing. (The arm motion during the backswing, by the way, should be used to help prepare the hips and trunk for their respective movements and to facilitate rhythm for the stroke.) When the arm is in its complete backswing position, it is externally rotated at the shoulder. As the forward swing takes place, the upper arm internally rotates at a high rate of speed.

Elbow Action

Movement at the elbow occurs next as the player accelerates the racquet head toward the point of impact. The view of Stan Smith's serve in Figure 8-9 shows the elbow action necessary for a good serve. Two types of motion are involved at the elbow: extension from the flexed position attained in the backswing and pronation (turning outward) of the hand and forearm. Velocities for these two movements are extremely high and, combined with its fragile structure, cause the joint to be quite vulnerable to injury. Therefore, as you develop this action, begin slowly until you get the feeling of what it should be like.

(a)   (b)

Figure 8-9(a), (b)   Watch how Stan Smith's elbow extends and how the shoulder and forearm rotate when ball impact is neared.

The Wrist Snap

Some teaching professionals feel that pronation is the last movement prior to ball contact on the serve and overhead. These instructors say that a wrist snap does not really occur until the ball has already been hit, as is often taught and professed. After impact much wrist flexion can be seen during the follow-through. Even though they feel that it doesn't happen prior to ball contact, these pros advocate that a tennis player think of using a wrist snap when developing the serve because it helps accelerate the racquet head through impact. They do, however, feel that when the player thinks *snap*, very little wrist action occurs while the hand and forearm actually pronate to bring the racquet through impact.

Other tennis instructors argue this point, saying that wrist hyperextension actually takes place during the latter stages of the backswing and in the early phases of the forward swing. Then, as the racquet head is accelerated toward impact, the hand flexes at the wrist until it is nearly straight relative to the forearm and actually snaps the racquet through impact into the flexed position. This debate has been predominant in many tennis circles where players discuss techniques or teaching pros converse about instructional methods. Little data has been previously provided that substantiates either opinion but the following information will show what some of my studies have revealed.

Using three-dimensional cinematography and an electronic device for measuring angular change, it was observed that wrist hyperextension did occur as the forward swing was begun. In addition, the wrist flexed from that hyperextended position through impact. It seems that elbow extension from the backscratch position, forearm pronation, and wrist movement occur at nearly the same time. To determine when each action takes place and how one contributes to the other would be near to impossible.

From the results of this research one can assume with a great deal of confidence that the teaching cue of using a wrist snap is not only valid from the standpoint of helping a player develop the serve more readily but also because the wrist snap actually does occur. I would not recommend, however, trying to consciously hyperextend and flex the wrist if you're trying to improve your serve. Just think of snapping the wrist and racquet through impact and you'll naturally accomplish what you're trying to do.

WHY DO SO MANY DIFFERENT SERVING TECHNIQUES EXIST?

When we discussed stroke form on the ground strokes, I said that due to the various grips available and the variety of swinging patterns a player could use, it really doesn't matter what they look like as long as the ball is hit correctly. When it comes to serving it seems that there are also a number of both efficient and inefficient methods.

Some of the various ways to serve effectively have recently come under severe scrutiny by professional teachers and are the topics of interesting debates. Although research has provided few actual answers, it may be of interest to discuss the mechanics of some of these movements, hoping to enlighten you about what the techniques can and cannot offer. To avoid being laborious, only three of the so-called efficient serving methods will be considered. These styles of serving involve: (1) allowing the hind foot to stay slightly behind and separate from the front foot in the serving motion versus allowing the hind foot to slide forward and take a position adjacent to the front foot, (2) landing first on the front foot versus landing on the hind foot following impact, and (3) using a full backswing method versus a half-swing method.

Service Footwork

The first technique to be studied deals with the footwork involved in serving. When watching the pros play, two basic types of foot movement can be seen: (1) where the hind foot stays separate from the front foot during the forward swing (Figure 8-10) and (2) where the hind foot is slid to a position adjacent to the front foot (as Chip Hooper demonstrates in Figure 8-11). During the discussion, it is necessary to

<table>
<tr><td align="center">(a)</td><td align="center">(b)</td></tr>
</table>

Figure 8-10(a), (b)   Notice how the hind foot stays separate from the front foot in the early part of the service motion only to be brought forward once ball contact is accomplished.

remember how important the hips are in serving and that the orientation of the feet will play a large role in how the ground-reaction force is transferred to and through the hips.

When the feet are kept separate during the serve (usually about shoulder width apart), they provide the player with a very stable base of support. This allows for an easy transfer of body momentum from the

Figure 8-11   Observe the positioning of the hind foot when Chip Hooper slides it forward during the early part of his serving motion.

Figure 8-12   This is John McEnroe's starting position when serving.

hind foot to the front foot. The position of the hind foot during the serving motion is the key to success using this technique. You've probably seen how McEnroe positions his feet when he begins his serving motion (Figure 8-12). His hind foot is placed quite far behind the front foot and he somewhat resembles a tightrope walker.

However, this is only a starting position. When McEnroe begins his forward motion, his hind foot swings forward to a position adjacent to the front foot. This helps to generate a great deal of hip rotation. Many players, especially juniors who like to imitate McEnroe's strokes, have a problem using this method because they usually keep the hind foot in a position where it blocks the hips from rotating effectively. If the hips are prevented from rotating, the serve will be poor. However, if the hind foot is positioned so the hips will be allowed to rotate or if the foot is swung forward, as McEnroe's is, then the hips can be used effectively.

Many skilled players slide their hind foot forward as they serve Figure 8-13). The biggest problem for those who use this technique is maintaining body stability. The better performers can slide the hind foot forward, stay fairly stable, and still generate a great deal of force from the ground. Some players who slide the hind foot forward often lose their balance because, when the hind foot is brought next to the front foot, a very small base of support is created. With balance being of great importance, an efficient service motion is often difficult to achieve. If stability doesn't seem to be a problem for a player, then a similar situation to the shoulder-width stance applies. If the hind foot is incorrectly slid forward so it is behind the front foot or is held in a fixed position (Figure 8-14), hip rotation will not be allowed. That's why most skilled players using this technique slide the hind foot slightly forward of the front foot allowing the hips to be open slightly and capable of optimal rotation during the stroke.

(a)   (b)

(c)   (d)

Figure 8-13(a), (b), (c), (d)   This athlete demonstrates how the hind foot can be slid forward when hitting a serve. Notice that it stays separate from the front foot in picture b and is slid forward to assist with the thrusting action in pictures c and d.

One yet to be determined point about these two methods of serving is: Which one provides the server with the most force possible for hitting with high velocity? Is it the service stance with the feet approximately shoulder width apart and with the body well-balanced or is it the position with both feet together allowing for the force from both legs to be applied to a very small area? The answer to this question is still unknown. At this point it seems that both positions may have certain advantages and disadvantages. I feel the selection of these techniques must be based on what is proper and comfortable relative to the needs and capabilities of each player.

Which foot should come through first? No matter which method of service footwork a tennis player uses, there is the problem of which foot comes through the motion the earliest to move into the court first. Some

Figure 8-14 Yvonne Vermak has a habit of lifting her hind leg during her service motion. This action is utilized by many players, but problems can exist if not performed exactly correctly. Balance is extremely difficult on only one foot and the amount of thrusting action is lowered since only one leg is used.

players allow the hind foot to come around during the service motion and lead the way into the court, as Brian Gottfried demonstrates in Figure 8-15, while others let the hind foot lag behind and lead the way into the court with the front foot, which Steve Denton does in Figure 8-16.

(a)   (b)

Figure 8-15(a), (b) Notice how Brian Gottfried's hind leg is allowed to rotate through the service motion so it leads the way into the tennis court.

(a)   (b)

Figure 8-16(a), (b)   Here Steve Denton's hind leg stays behind and the front foot is the first body part to land in the court.

It was commonly thought that the hardest serves would be hit by those using the crossover step and coming into the court with the hind foot first. The rationale behind this theory is that the hind foot being brought through so quickly facilitates usage of the hips and trunk because that leg helps the entire body rotate (Figure 8-17). This reasoning seems valid until you begin looking at some of the better serves in the game today. Tanner and McEnroe, for example, do not use a crossover movement but head into the court with the front foot first. The question now becomes this: If the two footwork motions do yield similar results, does the crossover step allow its user to get into the net faster when play-

Figure 8-17   Brian Gottfried demonstrates how the hind leg would come into the court first, possibly facilitating body rotation.

ing a serve-and-volley game? No evidence exists that dictates which method provides more force in the service nor is any data available to suggest which technique would get its performer to the net faster. At this time it can only be said that each technique has been used to hit high-velocity serves and that players using both of these footwork patterns have exhibited strong serve-and-volley games. Ongoing research may eventually provide some answers to these questions, but for now, selection of technique has to be up to the player and teacher.

The Debate over Arm Motion

The final controversial point to be discussed is the swinging motion in the serve. Although only a few basic methods exist that allow the player to hit a good serve, you would never guess it to be true while watching various players at your club or public park tennis courts. There almost seems to be a disease that dictates which idiosyncrasies a player will develop once the fundamental action of serving is learned. Interestingly enough, this disease is also seen in the pros. Tanner has a quick rotary action that requires incredibly accurate timing. Connors forms a *hook* with his wrist on the backswing that makes his serve conducive to high amounts of spin production. The list could go on indefinitely. However, two basic methods commonly seen will be discussed.

The most popular method of arm action in serving involves a full windmill-type swing (Figure 8-18). As the player takes a starting stance, the racquet is lowered so that it is almost pointing toward the ground. Then the racquet usually is brought up with an extended arm to a position of about shoulder height. From here the elbow flexes and the shoulder begins to rotate externally, allowing the racquet to be positioned behind the back (some call this a backscratching position). At this point, the linked system of the body has generated its force from the ground and is transferring it to the hips and trunk. The shoulder continues to rotate externally as the trunk rotates forward and, approximately when the trunk attains its maximum angular velocity, the shoulder accelerates its internal rotation to swing the racquet toward ball impact. As the racquet head is further accelerated, the elbow extends, the forearm pronates (turns outward), and the wrist flexes to provide the racquet with optimal impact velocity and to position it correctly for an effective ball contact.

The second method of arm action is quite similar except that instead of a full windmill-type swing (Figure 8-19), the technique is best described as a half-swing motion. The racquet, at the initiation of the swing, is not lowered so it is pointing toward the ground. Instead of dropping the racquet head to that position, the swinging arm merely rotates out to the side and goes immediately to the position where the

(a)   (b)

(c)   (d)   (e)

Figure 8-18(a), (b), (c), (d), (e) This tennis player demonstrates a windmill-type serving motion. Notice how the racquet is brought downward so it is pointing toward the ground (b) and also be aware that his front foot is the first foot contacting the court (e).

racquet is held with an extended arm at approximately shoulder height. From this point, everything is the same as with the full-swing technique in terms of movements, the generation of force, and the transfer of that force to the racquet.

Some authorities have argued that a difference does exist between the two serving methods with regard to the amount of momentum produced during each swing. Most of the debate states that the half-swing method doesn't permit usage of the entire body to hit the serve in the most efficient manner. Others say that the main difference between the two serving types is rhythm. They feel that the half-swing technique doesn't allow the player to achieve a definite rhythm to time the succession of events in the body's linked chain system properly.

(a)   (b)

(c)   (d)   (e)

Figure 8-19(a), (b), (c), (d), (e)   Observe the difference when utilizing
a half-swing serving motion. Notice that the racquet is brought
almost straight back from his starting position (a) to a position where
it almost faces the back fence (b). In addition, observe that his hind
foot is the first foot contacting the court following impact.

It's difficult to say whether any difference in the generation of
momentum is present between the two stroke patterns. From a purely
biomechanical sense there should not be. However, there may be a
definite variation of rhythm between the two strokes. For example, do
you remember when you took serving lessons as a beginner? Your

teacher probably told you that if you tossed the ball poorly you didn't have to swing at the ball (which is definitely how an improper toss should be handled). However, if you did go ahead and swing the racquet, you could use the backswing to regulate the velocity of the entire movement. If the ball was tossed too high or if wind conditions prevented a normal swing, the backswing could be slightly slowed and regulated to generate momentum effectively. The backswing in both serving methods can be regulated but obviously there is more leeway for stroke accommodation using the full-swing method. Regardless of that, however, it seems that the two service motions can be utilized effectively and their selection would depend on personal preference.

WHY DO SOME PLAYERS SERVE AND HIT OVERHEADS BETTER THAN OTHERS?

As I said earlier, serving and hitting an overhead is similar to an overhand throw in baseball (Figure 8-20). In fact, many sport scientists have shown that a throwing action is an absolute necessity in a championship serve or overhead, which is probably why some players have better serves than others. They simply use a more efficient throwing motion, which causes the players to utilize the linked system most effectively. Therefore, let's see where some athletes go wrong in their throwing action.

As you are aware the primary source of power on a serve and overhead is the ground. The generated force is transferred through the legs to

(a)   (b)   (c)

Figure 8-20(a), (b), (c) Compare the actions of these athletes when hitting a serve (a), hitting an overhead smash (b), and throwing in an overhand motion (c). Similar body actions occur for each maneuver.

the hips and on to the trunk and upper limb. If a problem exists in the force transmission between any of these key body parts, the serve won't be nearly as effective. The one body segment that contributes to most service difficulties is the hips. Many performers don't employ the hips very well on the serve or overhead.

Surprisingly, many competitors, when describing their own service form, feel that their body becomes a long lever stretched out over the baseline at impact. It's not unusual to hear them say something similar to: "I look just like Roscoe Tanner when I hit the ball." The problem is that they really do feel their service motion resembles Tanner's when in fact it doesn't. Instead of using a proper throwing type motion that involves hip and trunk rotation, these players tend to flex the hips and force the trunk forward to hit a hard serve. Interestingly enough this action of serving resembles one of the developmental stages of a mature throwing pattern. An analysis of the various stages of developing an overhand throw may help you if your serve isn't as effective as you like.

Developing a Sound Throwing Action

When individuals (particularly children) first learn to throw, they utilize only arm movement to propel the ball. Realizing sooner or later that this motion alone won't propel the ball very far, and also by modeling better throwers, these people will adopt a throwing pattern that involves a forceful forward flexion of the trunk. Somewhere during this process novice throwers begin to step forward with the opposite foot as the transfer of linear momentum is developed. Finally they will acquire the proper skills necessary to coil the body segments, step forward, and uncoil the body parts as they learn to combine linear and angular momentum effectively.

Similar stages of body movement can be seen in the serve and overhead, the most predominant being where the trunk is forcefully flexed forward. Tennis players guilty of this can easily flex and extend the knees, but when the force nears its transfer to the hips they can't coordinate the action. Instead of adequately rotating the hips, they block the hips (prevent them from rotating) by keeping the hind leg fixed to the ground or in the air behind the body. Jimmy Connors, seen in Figure 8-21, is one player who performs this way. The only way Connors can hit a hard first serve is to forcefully flex his trunk forward. Players such as Connors often can hit a fairly hard serve, but it's still not as good as it could be if the linked system were properly coordinated. To see if this applies to you have your serve and overhead videotaped and watch the replay in slow motion. If your hips stick out backward toward the fence and your body is bent a great deal (a slight bend is all right), you may want to work on your overhand throwing action and apply the motion to your strokes.

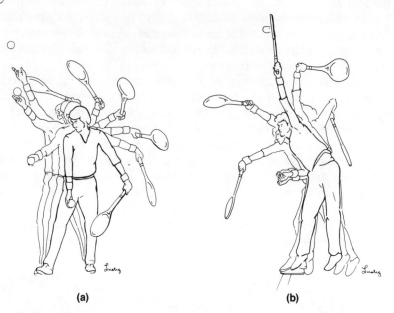

(a)   **(b)**

Figure 8-21(a), (b)   Notice how Jimmy Connors' service motion resembles that of any other player in picture a but how his hind leg has been prevented from rotating toward the court in picture b and how the trunk has been flexed forward forcefully at the hips.

The Service Hitch

Some people can employ all their body segments correctly but have such poor timing that they have a delay, or hitch, in their service motion. This hitch can occur at any point in the serve but occurs most often when the racquet gets in the backscratch position (Figure 8-22). Several things may cause a hitch in a service motion, but the most common is poor timing between the tossing action of the ball and the swing of the racquet. Many players use a very high toss and a quick backswing motion so that by the time the racquet is ready for the forward swing, the ball still isn't near the position of impact. Therefore, a delay in the swinging action must occur. This delay has more significance than that of merely slowing down the entire movement.

Remember why the backswing is used? First, it *sets* the body by coiling the hips and trunk backward in preparation for the forward swing. Second, it helps a player to establish a rhythm for gaining momentum into the stroke and readying the shoulder and elbow joints for the upward and forward acceleration of the racquet. For these reasons a hitch in the serve severely reduces the effectiveness of a service motion. In fact, the inefficiency of movement is so great that the player

Figure 8-22 This is the position where the majority of service hitches occur.

using this motion may as well begin the service motion at the location of the hitch rather than go through the other preparatory movements. The preliminary actions in the backswing become meaningless because of the way the hitch cuts down the generation of momentum. However, when starting a service motion from a backscratch position it is highly improbable that the service velocity will be as great.

Jumping into the Serve

As skilled tennis players attempt to hit high-velocity serves, they often come off the ground during the motion. Some authorities say that a good server actually jumps into the serve (Figure 8-23). In fact, some teaching pros have analyzed slow-motion movies detailing the service motions of highly-skilled players at world championship cannonball serving contests. It was reported that those players who hit the fastest serves all jumped off the court. Frequently, the higher the jump, the faster the serve. From a biomechanical standpoint, it makes sense that the faster the serve, the higher off the ground a player might go. However, it is extremely doubtful that the players actually jump into the serve, especially to reach any particular height at which a peak racquet velocity might be met. To attempt a purposeful and forceful upward jump when serving would require a unique amount of coordination, and inhibit the tennis player's attempt to hit an effective serve. Therefore, a leaping action seen during the serves of many world-class competitors shouldn't be looked upon as a necessity for hitting a good serve. These players, you see, generate so much momentum (both linear and angular) that the jumping action is the result of all the force created to hit a hard serve. If any of those players consciously jumped into their serve, the results would be less than optimal.

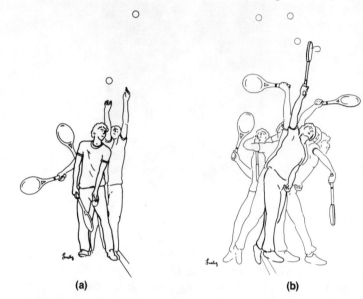

Figure 8-23(a), (b)   Notice how Ivan Lendl is off the ground during his service motion (b). Be aware that this is not a forceful jump but that he is actually pulling his body off the ground due to the thrusting and throwing action.

Use of the Opposite Arm

No matter how much force is acquired from the ground and transferred through the body, one very important maneuver takes place to transmit a final thrust of force in accelerating the upper limb. When watching the next pro match on television, watch a player's opposite arm action during the serve or overhead.

The nonswinging arm never does come completely around to the side during the motion, but the elbow travels to the side and the forearm suddenly tucks in front and quickly positions itself across the lower chest wall (Figure 8-24). This motion contradicts many teaching techniques because it happens so fast that few people ever see it. By now you must be wondering why it takes place. A good example might be for you to recall what it was like in the high school locker room when you flipped someone with a towel or someone flipped you. How did the person flipping the towel make it pop so loudly? What happens is that the hand develops a high forward velocity and quickly pulls the towel along with it. The hand slows down and, as the towel passes by the hand, the hand forcefully accelerates backward. This pulls one end of the towel backward while the other end is still moving forward. The result is a loud snap

(a) (b)

Figure 8-24(a), (b)   Notice how the opposite arm follows the trunk around (a) and suddenly tucks in front of the trunk across the chest wall (b) during the service motion. This acts as a braking mechanism to decelerate the trunk rotation allowing the upper limb to accelerate.

which means that, if the towel is aimed correctly, it can really inflict some pain. Realistically, the human body and its movements are not as simply explained as the motion of the towel. However, there are some similarities that can be applied to serving and to hitting a smash.

As the trunk attains a high rotary velocity and the racquet approaches the position from which it will be accelerated forward, the opposite arm comes across the front of the trunk. The opposite arm, acting as a brake, quickly decelerates the trunk and causes the upper limb to snap forward, somewhat like the towel. This elastic reaction provides the racquet with a high velocity.

Should You Jump to Hit an Overhead Smash?

Should you jump to hit an overhead? Many of the students that I work with feel that they should jump into every overhead they hit. I'm not sure of the exact reason for this, unless they feel more powerful when airborne. Whatever the reason for jumping, you should never jump unless you are forced to. When you hit an overhead with both feet on the ground as shown by Peter Fleming and by Bernie Mitton in Figure 8-25, your body is extremely stable. Once you are airborne, as Bernie Mitton is in Figure 8-26, you have no control over your body's flight path. In essence, your body becomes a projectile. This means that you will follow

(a)   (b)

(c)   (d)

Figure 8-25(a), (b), (c), (d)   Peter Fleming (a, b, and c) and Bernie
Mitton (d) demonstrate the stability gained when hitting an overhead
while in contact with the ground.

a predetermined flight (however small it may be), causing a potential
problem with balance and timing for the stroke.

One question I always receive is "How is a ground-reaction force
involved when a player must jump to hit an overhead smash?" To
answer this question I should first say that a ground-reaction force
definitely does play a role in the jump overhead. When the athlete
realizes he or she must leave the ground to reach and effectively hit an
overhead smash (Figure 8-27) the body must first be turned sideways to
the net (somewhat like the initial serving stance). When the ball nears the
player the knee of the hind leg flexes and extends forcefully, pushing the
athlete off the ground. The extension of the hind leg initiates a ground-

Figure 8-26   Often you must jump to reach and hit a high overhead smash as Bernie Mitton is demonstrating.

reaction force that is transferred to the hips and trunk just prior to leaving the ground. Some of the force generated from the ground is lost when the competitor leaps off the court, but enough remains and is transferred to the upper limb, allowing for a high racquet velocity.

The competitor should remember several things about a jump overhead before attempting one. First, once you leave the ground you have

Figure 8-27   In this figure representation of Jimmy Connors' overhead he demonstrates how to make your body a long lever and to use good body rotation when hitting a jump overhead.

absolutely no control over the trajectory your body will follow until it reaches the court again. Therefore, stability in hitting a jump overhead is of extreme necessity. You must maintain good control over the various body parts involved so that once you are airborne you can swing the racquet efficiently. The second point to bring up is that of control. Since upper-body control is so important, it is suggested that you don't try to hit a jump overhead with high velocity. In slowing down your stroke a bit you will optimize your shot control. In my opinion, shot control is much more important than stroke velocity when you develop your jump overhead. Third, a jump overhead is not recommended unless it is absolutely necessary. When your feet maintain contact with the court surface you are in the most stable position possible, facilitating not only shot control but allowing you to develop greater velocity on the stroke.

Hitting with Control

The production of racquet head speed is only one part of hitting an effective serve or overhead. The second part is control. Many players feel that because their racquets are so high above the net at ball contact, they must hit downward to keep the ball in play. They don't realize that even the most skilled tennis players have difficulty hitting downward and keeping the ball in play. In fact, it is a fairly well-accepted fact that a player must have a reach of nearly 11 ft with the racquet and hit a flat serve at almost 100 mph just to hit downward $3°$ from the horizontal. Gravity and wind resistance have a tremendous effect on a flying object (like a tennis ball) once it's been struck. That's why most players who hit downward end up putting their serves and overheads into the net. The downward descent of the ball, combined with the effects of gravity, cause the ball to end up in the net. It is for this reason that most good servers hit the ball straight out or slightly upward from the racquet face even when hitting very high-velocity serves.

THE SECOND SERVE

It's been said that a tennis player is only as good as his or her second serve. This makes a lot of sense if you consider that the opponent is usually expecting a high-velocity ball on the first serve. When you miss it, your opponent gains a big psychological advantage awaiting your second serve, which obviously won't be as hard. Therefore, it is a necessity for any tournament player to not only work on achieving a high level of consistency in first serves, but also to develop an effective second serve. The first thing you should be aware of about the second serve is that the racquet head velocity is often faster than it is during a first serve. This may seem confusing as the ball travels so much faster on a first serve. However, the key point in hitting a good second serve is that the ball must have a great deal of spin (usually a combination of sidespin and topspin) to control its flight. This means that the racquet must not only provide the ball with a great deal of forward impetus (although not as much as a first serve), but it must also quickly brush the back side of ball to give it

(a)

(b)

(c)   (d)   (e)

Figure 8-28(a), (b), (c), (d), (e)   This athlete is illustrating how to hit an effective second serve. The goal of a good second serve is to hit the ball deep into the opponent's service court and with enough spin to maximize control.

rotation. Therefore, the racquet movement on a second serve doesn't move forward as quickly as a first serve, but because of the much faster vertical movement required for spin production, the overall racquet velocity is often higher.

To develop a penetrating second serve it is important that you attempt to hit the ball with at least three-fourths of the speed of your first serve. As the second serve is hit try to place some amount of topspin on the ball (it is difficult to hit pure topspin on a serve but a combination of topspin and sidespin should not be too difficult). The competitor in Figure 8-28 demonstrates how a good second serve should be hit. You can compare this motion with his first serve, which was demonstrated earlier. Be aware that his ball toss is not as far in toward the court and that the ball is also located more above his head at impact than it was for his first serve. This type of ball toss facilitates the necessary spin production. When you practice this action, be sure to work on (1) ball velocity, (2) spin production, and (3) depth into the service box. A short second serve (any serve in front half of your opponent's service box) will only bring you more trouble.

SUMMARY

It should now be obvious why the serve and overhead are among the most important strokes in the game of tennis. With the many people playing and the different methods of hitting a ball, it is no wonder confusion often arises when discussing the correct method of serving or hitting an overhead. It is essential to understand that the force generated in hitting an effective serve and overhead must come from the ground and that the force must be efficiently transferred through the body to the racquet. In addition, once that force is transferred to the upper limb, it is important to concentrate on snapping the wrist through impact. This controversy has existed for years, but now seems to be more understood.

You should also be aware that an overhead smash isn't necessary every time a ball is above your head. As Vitas Gerulaitus shows in Figure 8-29, a high volley may be called for. This is especially true under two circumstances: (1) when the ball simply isn't high enough to use the proper mechanics for an overhead and (2) when you haven't gotten into the correct position under the ball. So don't try to overpower every high ball. There are times when you must volley the ball deep and wait for your next chance at a smash.

Although much has been discussed about how the human body hits a serve and overhead, it's still very important that you realize that the only way to excel is to receive the proper instruction and to practice the method you are taught. Many people feel that they perform the serve and

Figure 8-29   There will be times when you must decide to hit either an overhead smash or a high volley. As Vitas Gerulaitis demonstrates, when you cannot hit an overhead smash efficiently you should use a high volley. A poor overhead in this position could hurt you but a penetrating high volley can be very effective.

overhead in an optimum manner—until they see themselves on film or videotape. When that occurs the reaction is usually "is that me?" Therefore, no matter how good you consider your serve or overhead you may want to have a knowledgeable teaching pro critique them so you won't have to say "do I really hit the ball like that?" any more.

It's a Game
of Continuous
Dire Emergencies

GLOSSARY

Approach Shot — The intermediary stroke that helps you go from a position behind the baseline to the net.

Backhand Overhead — A stroke often utilized to hit a high shot over the backhand side of your body.

Lob — A shot hit with a high trajectory deep into the opponent's court.

Service Return — The stroke used to return an opponent's serve.

Peter Burwash, a renowned tennis instructor, has used the word *emergency* when speaking of the game of tennis. One of Peter's favorite stories is of the time he competed against Arthur Ashe in a tournament in the late 1960s. Instead of being on the offensive, as any skilled player would like to be, Peter found himself in a state of continuous emergency. Ashe easily had him running from side to side and from front court to back court. The interesting thing is that almost any tennis player has run into the situation where they're playing someone who seems to be in total control of the match. In fact, you never know what's going to happen next in any tennis match! With every movement of the opponent, you have to make adjustments in your own strategy and court position.

One mark of a great player is not only to be able to hit various spins, low hard drives, and soft looping moonballs. but to be able to receive each of these shots and counter what the opponent has done. With that in mind, we need to examine some of the emergencies you might encounter in match play and how you can most efficiently react to each.

THE RETURN OF SERVE

At the initiation of every point in a match, a player is immediately placed in an emergency as he or she must return the serve. Not having any idea how the opponent will hit the serve, an athlete must be prepared to react to its placement and velocity. You never know if the opponent will swing you wide with a heavy slice, blast a ball right at you, or hit a kick serve to the middle. Therefore, to hit an effective return you must be able to read the velocity of the opponent's serve and the type of ball spin it has. You can refer to the chapters on the serve and ball spin to help you with this aspect, but we should discuss why some players make service return mistakes and how you can improve your own return of serve.

Although most tournament competitors have extremely good eye-racquet coordination, they often don't hit their service returns very well. Obviously, this may have something to do with how well the opponent is serving, but it's not unusual to see poor returns of poor serves. The main reason is that when hitting a return many players don't have their racquets properly positioned at impact. Then there are other players who hold the racquet in the correct position but have little force behind the return. One phrase fits all of these athletes very well: They let the ball play off their racquet instead of the racquet playing the ball.

To hit an offensive return of serve you must attack the ball (see Figure 9-1). This is true regardless of the return you wish to hit, whether it's a hard drive or a soft underspin return. If you don't think of being aggressive on any return, you're likely to mistime your swing and hit the ball poorly. A few coaching cues I've used in the past may help you to achieve an offensive return.

First, watch how the opponent stands when preparing to serve. If he or she lines up in an open stance (Figure 9-2), a slice serve is a strong possibility. If a closed stance is assumed, as in Figure 9-3, a kick serve may be hit. Be aware, however, that the more skilled a player is the better the athlete can disguise these shots, so this strategy only works on less skilled players.

The next point is timing your first movement for hitting a return of serve. Assume your ready position near the baseline. As a rule of thumb,

(a)   (b)

Figure 9-1(a), (b) This is how John McEnroe often attacks his return of serve. Regardless of his body mechanics, observe how his racquet has contacted the ball well in front of his body. While many players have better body mechanics, their racquet heads are late getting to the proper contact point.

stand about 3–4 ft behind the baseline if the opponent has a hard serve and at the baseline if the serve is mediocre. As the opponent takes his or her backswing, concentrate intently on the ball. Once the forward swing has begun, take a short, balanced hop forward, as John McEnroe demonstrates in Figure 9-4. It is important that you maintain total body control during this small hopping action. Don't jump too much or move forward too quickly. The purpose of the hop is to obtain linear momentum

Figure 9-2 This would be the view if the opponent would prepare to serve from an open stance. Notice how the hips are almost too open toward the court even before he has begun his backswing.

Figure 9-3 This is what a closed serving stance would resemble. Notice the position of his hind leg which would allow the coiling action of the hips and trunk during his backswing.

in your return. Try to time the landing of the hop so that your feet hit the ground when the opponent contacts the ball. In this way, you gain linear momentum forward and *set* the lower limb muscles to move one way or the other.

Immediately upon recognizing which side of your body the ball is traveling toward, use the unit turn to take the racquet back in a slightly shorter backswing than usual. The unit turn allows you to coil your body for the stroke and the short backswing will enable you to swing the racquet forward quickly. This is the most crucial point in your return. As shown in Figure 9-5, think of getting the racquet to the impact point

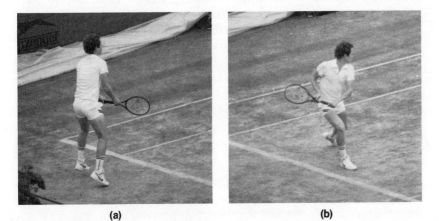

(a)   (b)

Figure 9-4(a), (b) Notice how John McEnroe takes a hop forward, preparing to react to the opponent's serve. The unit turn is employed so linear and angular momentum can be used.

(a)   (b)   (c)

Figure 9-5(a), (b), (c) Observe how this tennis player hops forward to hit an aggressive service return but maintains control over her upper body during the stroke.

quickly—but don't lift up as you swing. If at this point you're lazy the racquet won't be oriented properly at contact. Finish your swing with a good follow-through and move to a court position that prepares you for your opponent's next shot.

There are basically two types of returns (besides a lob) you can hit: (1) a deep drive in which you hit and stay near your own baseline or (2) a shot hit short into the opponent's court. Either can be hit flat, with topspin, or with underspin. The purpose of a deep drive could be to keep the opponent on the defensive behind his or her baseline, to pull the opponent out of position by hitting crosscourt, or to go for a clean winner. The short return could be used to bring a baseliner to the net, to hit at the feet of a serve and volleyer, or to go for an outright winner by angling the ball crosscourt. It is important to remember that either type of return can be followed to the net if you can take the offensive more readily against your opponent. One method of practicing service returns is to have your practice partner stand at his/her service line and hit serves into various parts of your service box. Speeds and spins can be varied to simulate first and second serves so you learn to react, move, and hit effective returns quickly.

MUST YOU ALWAYS HIT A BACKHAND?

Once the return is in play and the point is in progress, many players find themselves struggling as the opponent continually attacks their backhands. Besides working to improve their backhand, there is another thing these players should always bear in mind. There will be times when the opponent won't hit a penetrating drive to the backhand side of the court. For whatever the reason, he or she will occasionally hit a soft floater or lob. If this happens to you, be aware that you don't have to hit a backhand.

Whenever you get the chance, feel free to run around your backhand and return the ball with a forehand (Figure 9-6). Not only will this make you a more offensive player, it will make your opponent think twice about hitting a soft shot to your backhand.

If the opponent hits a high lob to your backhand, you have two alternatives: (1) to run around your backhand and hit a conventional

(a)   (b)

(c)   (d)   (e)

Figure 9-6(a), (b), (c), (d), (e)   Observe how this athlete handles a softly hit ball to his backhand side. You see him quickly maneuver around the ball so he can hit an aggressive forehand drive.

overhead smash or (2) hit a backhand overhead. The same stroke mechanics as described in Chapter 8 should be used for the conventional overhead. The only difference is that quick lateral footwork is necessary to run around your backhand.

To hit a backhand overhead, timing is of extreme importance. You must turn your body sideways to the net (Figure 9-7), internally rotate the upper limb so the racquet is placed over the shoulder, step toward the net or jump (whichever is required by the shot), and externally rotate the arm to hit the ball straight out from the racquet head. Since this is naturally a weak stroking movement, the skilled player will practice it in order to enhance timing and control and to help make it a forceful shot. If you wish to practice it be sure to work on control first. You should be able to direct the ball down the line as well as crosscourt. Once control is properly developed you can work on timing to hit a powerful shot.

THE APPROACH SHOT

Unless you're the type of player who sets up camp at the baseline during a point, you need to be aware of how to get to the net most effectively. One way is to serve and volley but another, and very important maneuver, is to hit an approach shot and go to the net. When the opponent hits a ball near your service line, it usually acts as your personal invitation to the net. But here is where many players run into problems. They prepare to hit the approach and, because of improper mechanics, they make errors and lose points.

(a)   (b)   (c)

Figure 9-7(a), (b), (c) This tennis player demonstrates the mechanics of hitting a backhand overhead when forced to leap in the air for the smash.

They either continue to lose points by trying to approach the net in any way they can, or they pitch a tent at the baseline and leave only when the opponent has hit short. Immediately upon hitting the return of the short ball, they retreat to their baseline sanctuary. We discussed why it's so important to go to the net in Chapter 7, so now let's talk about how to get there.

Any time your opponent hits a ball short into your court (short refers to anything near the service line or closer to the net), it can serve as your personal invitation to the net. All you need to do is hit an approach shot and follow it to a strategic net position where you can be more offensive. Although many players realize the value of going to the net they have difficulty in doing so because they have poor approach shots. However, the problem may not be in the approach shot itself but in how the players react to the opponent's stroke and move to hit the approach shot.

Before describing the mechanics of an approach shot, I shall discuss two extremely important factors. First, you should always be aware of how the ball comes off the opponent's racquet. During practice watch your partner's strokes carefully and, as a ball is hit, try to immediately recognize where it is going, how hard it is hit, and what type of spin it has on it. This will help you get a good jump on a short shot so that you can approach the net. The second thing you should always try to do is to never let the ball drop too low before hitting your approach shot. The lower the ball is the more upward you must hit to clear the net. The ideal point of contact is between waist and shoulder height but if the ball doesn't bounce that high try to hit it at the peak of its bounce. However, you must be sure your body is under control as you run toward the ball.

The traditional teaching expression was never hit an approach on the run because you aren't balanced and will lose control. This idiom is now almost out of date. Although it's true that you don't want to be sprinting into the approach shot, you can move through it and still be in control of your body. The most stable position in which to hit the approach shot would be for you to be stopped, but that slows your process in getting to the net and a step or two closer to the net can be crucial. Therefore, a current expression used to describe approaching the net is to *glide* through the stroke. As the athlete in Figure 9-8 shows, by keeping the body a bit lower than usual to maintain stability and by turning slightly sideways a player can stride into the shot and hit deep, effective approaches. The sideways turn of the body will be greater for the backhand (especially the one-handed backhand) because of the orientation of the racquet arm to the body. That's why you may see some players crisscrossing their steps to hit a one-handed backhand approach shot. This allows them to turn the body sideways to the net yet permits gliding (via the crisscross steps) through the shot. This footwork is usually not seen for the forehand (see Figure 9-9) because the orientation of the racquet arm

(a)   (b)   (c)

Figure 9-8(a), (b), (c)   Here you can see the footwork and stroking pattern necessary to hit a backhand approach shot. Following contact with the ball (c), the athlete will continue to move through the shot toward the net.

to the body doesn't mandate the side turn. However, a player will usually turn slightly sideways to facilitate the forehand swing but the crisscross stepping will not be as obvious.

Regardless of how far sideways a player turns to hit the approach shot or how they chose to glide through the shot, the largest problem in body movement occurs in the middle of the stroke. Most players, as they hit approach shots, find themselves near the sideline of the court as few of the opponent's shots will be hit to the middle. Realizing they are not in the middle of the court, they feel that there is extreme urgency to recover from the approach shot and quickly get to midcourt. The problem is that

(a)   (b)

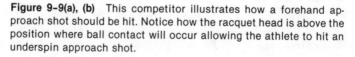

Figure 9-9(a), (b)   This competitor illustrates how a forehand approach shot should be hit. Notice how the racquet head is above the position where ball contact will occur allowing the athlete to hit an underspin approach shot.

they do it too soon. Many players are going to midcourt before they ever hit the ball (Figure 9-10). They pull away from the approach shot too soon, causing their body to become unstable and resulting in an errant stroke. The body must stay into the approach shot at least until the ball has been hit. One cue I give the players I work with is mentally to draw a straight line between their shoulders. As they prepare to hit a backhand approach shot, I ask them to keep that line directed toward the point of impact until the ball has been hit. Once contact has occurred, they can move into position for the opponent's return. There is usually plenty of time to attain an advantageous position for your next shot.

In the preceding discussion and photographs you've only been exposed to approach shots hit with underspin. A controversy exists among many athletes as to whether a player should hit an approach shot with topspin or underspin. There are authorities who prefer all topspin approaches, others who advocate hitting all underspin approach shots, and still another group favoring that approach shots above the net be hit with topspin and those below the net be hit with underspin. Wherever you stand on this issue, there are a few biomechanical facts to consider. First, remember that topspin can only be hit with low-to-high acceleration of the racquet head and that balls below the top of the net will most likely have to be hit with a slightly opened racquet face to propel the ball upward to clear the net. Therefore, the player attempting to hit a topspin approach shot on a ball below the net may have his work cut out for him. First, the racquet face must be slightly open. This by itself creates a huge problem for the topspin approach shot because, with an open racquet face, the low-to-high acceleration of the racquet head may cause the ball to go long. These two factors, combined with the fact that to get below the ball for creating topspin when it is already below net level and closer to the net than usual, make a topspin approach shot in this situation

Figure 9-10 This tennis player shows the *wrong* way to hit an approach shot. Observe how his body is already moving toward the center of the court as the ball is being hit.

quite difficult even for advanced competitors. In addition, the topspin approach shot often causes the athlete, while trying to accelerate the racquet head upward, to lift the body excessively and create even more problems for the stroke.

An advantage of the topspin approach is that it can be hit with a great deal of velocity, especially from net height or above. The problem here is that if there is not enough topspin placed on the ball it might travel long and if too much spin is placed on the ball it may bounce too short in the court to be effective. The argument here, of course, is that the ball will jump off the court and cause problems for the opponent trying to hit a good passing shot.

Underspin can also be used to cause the ball to jump off the court, but in a different way. Hit with a low trajectory, the underspin approach shot will skid, stay low, and force the opponent to hit up on the passing shot. This skidding action of the underspin approach is one of the reasons I prefer teaching this shot. The naturally bevelled racquet face required to hit underspin, combined with the necessary high-to-low motion, allows the underspin approach to be hit when the ball is in any position on the court. It usually cannot be hit with the high velocity that topspin can because of an underspin shot's tendency to float, but it can be hit as a low, deep drive which lowers the opponent's chances of hitting an easy winner. The biggest disadvantage of the underspin approach shot is that if the ball is hit lazily and has a higher than normal trajectory the ball will sit up, allowing a great opportunity for an offensive shot from the opponent and creating a new tennis emergency for yourself.

WHEN THE OPPONENT IS AT THE NET

Just as you work on your game to hit on the run and to hit effective approach shots, so does almost every opponent you'll ever face. They also know how to get to the net effectively, presenting you with yet another emergency: getting the ball by the opponent.

When an opponent takes the net against you there are basically four things you can do: (1) hit a passing shot down the line, (2) hit a passing shot crosscourt, (3) hit the ball right at the opponent, attempting to catch him/her off guard, or (4) lob over the opponent's head.

As you attempt to pass a net player, the obvious goal is to hit the ball so that it clears the opponent's lateral reach. The ball must be hit hard enough so it can get by the person before he/she reaches it but, just as importantly, it must be an accurate shot. You should realize that when your opponent reaches the net there is little time to think about what must happen. Each passing shot you hit depends on the velocity and placement of your opponent's stroke and where the opponent is located relative to where your passing shot will be hit. It takes a great deal of experience before a tennis player learns the proper stroke mechanics to use in various situations. I suggest that you actually practice your passing shots. Have your practice partner volley at the net. Both of you hit a couple of balls directly to the partner. The volleyer should hit his/her third ball to either side (not trying for a winner) of your court. From here, play out the point. You get to work on your passing shots and, if you're unsuccessful, your partner gets to practice hitting volley winners. You can even expand the drill so that the player in the backcourt can lob also, which will make the practice more realistic. Just remember a few things about hitting a passing shot:

1. You don't need to go for the line every time. If you aim a couple of feet inside the lines, you'll usually win the point but you'll also give yourself some margin for error.

2. Use your opponent as a target from which to hit away. By attempting to hit your shots around the opponent, you'll find your accuracy quickly improving.

3. Play the percentages on your passing shots and don't try for extreme angles.

The lob is another alternative you have when your opponent is at the net. In fact, the lob may be the most underrated shot in tennis. It can be used to change the pace of play during a point or to give you more time to recover to a strategic court position when you've been pulled out of court, but it is especially effective when the opponent is at the net. You can hit a defensive lob that is basically hit to move the opponent away from the net and into his or her backcourt or you can hit an offensive lob where you are actually going for a winner.

The defensive lob is usually hit with underspin (Figure 9-11) which allows the player more control and will also give the ball a bit more lift. A bevelled racquet face is necessary while using a low-to-high swinging motion. The goal is to give the ball a high trajectory, clearing the opponent's reach, and hitting the ball deep into the opponent's court, forcing him or her away from the net.

The offensive lob, seen in Figure 9-12, can also be hit with underspin but is generally hit with topspin. The topspin causes the ball to have a looping trajectory as it clears the opponent's reach plus causes the ball to pick up its horizontal velocity after the bounce.

Although many people feel the topspin lob is extremely difficult to hit, it doesn't have to be. Good timing is required, but you should think of a topspin lob as being a modified ground stroke. For example, try hitting your normal topspin ground stroke with a practice partner. As you get a rally going, work on increasing the net clearance of your shots. You

Figure 9–11(a), (b) The defensive lob must be hit with slight under-spin. Observe the bevelled racquet face sending the ball upward.

may have to slow down your shot a bit but don't try to hit any more topspin. Keep working on increased net clearance until your shots are going about 20 ft above the net. Once you've gotten the feeling of this stroking movement, remember it, because you've just learned how to hit an effective topspin lob.

Figure 9–12(a), (b), (c) Here you can see how a tournament player hits an offensive lob with topspin. Observe the steep low-to-high motion of the racquet head.

One shortcoming of hitting the lob is that if you hit it short the opponent will be able to reach it and hit an offensive shot. Many players, once they realize they have hit a poor lob, give up and let the opponent hit whatever he or she wishes. However, you will very seldom see a great player give up in such an instance, especially during a big point. If a ball is hit short, the elite competitor will wait until the last second (usually just as the opponent prepares to swing at the ball) and then sprint toward one side of the court. Trying to second guess the opponent in these situations can have big payoffs because you can often obtain a great deal of psychological momentum by returning a ball the opponent assumed was a clean winner. Therefore, don't stay in the middle waiting for the opponent's shot when you send over what's called a *duck ball*. You must go one way or the other. At least that way you will have a chance to get your racquet on the ball.

SUMMARY

Interestingly enough, the better your skills become, the more emergencies you'll see yourself in. How well you react to each emergency and accommodate your own movements relative to the situation will determine if you will continue to excel.

If I were to suggest anything to help you improve along these lines, it would be the following: First, always try to maintain body balance regardless of the shot you must hit. Second, be sure to play the percentages whenever possible. Know your limitations and go for shots you're capable of hitting while avoiding the extremes. If you don't own a shot, don't hit it.

Finally, be a flexible tennis player. You must be not only willing to adapt to different match play situations, but you must be able to react and perform relative to what your opponent does. This is a major step on the way to championship tennis.

CHAPTER **10**

Are You Ready
for Championship
Tennis?

Now that you've been exposed to the effects of sports science on the game of tennis, with specific emphasis placed on improving your game, where do you go from here? Are you ready to go into competition implementing some of the things I've discussed or, if you're not ready, how will you know when you are? Although the answer to this question is difficult to determine, I'd like to summarize some of the major topics in the book and combine them with a few general coaching tips. As you go through each area, always apply what is said to yourself and your game. In that way I think you'll be able to improve your game most efficiently.

BE IN CONTROL AND LET YOUR RACQUET DO THE WORK

When playing competitive tennis, many athletes become so intent on hitting high-velocity shots that they literally put their entire body into the stroke by jumping as they swing (see Figure 10-1). Not only isn't this necessary, but when the entire body is used incorrectly (as it is when jumping into a stroke), loss of control will result. Therefore, I suggest that you think of driving only your tennis racquet into the ball at impact. Remember that your racquet is the only part that hits the ball while the rest of your body merely supplies the force. So, when you prepare to hit a

Figure 10-1 Even though John McEnroe has left the ground during this backhand drive, he has excellent control over his racquet head. Notice that his shoulders are level and that impact will occur well ahead of the body.

powerful stroke, don't let your body go out of control as it is your power supply. Imagine your racquet driving through the ball at impact.

MAKE THINGS HAPPEN DURING A POINT

When people enter the competitive levels of tennis, they tend to become extremely tentative when playing points. They often go on the defensive and hope that the opponent will make a mistake. You should be aware that you cannot wait for something to happen in championship tennis (see Figure 10-2)! Yes, some players attain a certain level of success by

Figure 10-2 Never let it be said that Jimmy Connors plays a tentative game of tennis. His relentless and aggressive style of play serves as an example for many tournament tennis players.

staying at the baseline, retrieving all of the opponent's shots, and waiting for an error. However, for you to excel in the higher levels of tennis, you must learn to make things happen—not to wait for them to happen. You can do this by thinking aggressively and attacking the opponent's weaknesses when the opportunity arises. However, don't go overboard with aggression and allow your stroking actions to go out of control.

HITTING SHOTS YOU OWN

In the heat of competition, many players will attempt to hit low percentage shots that, once the point is over, they know they should never have tried (see Figure 10-3). In the elite levels of tennis this is called being able to hit the shots that you own. For example, when you're in a certain position on the court, don't attempt to hit an extremely difficult shot but try your best to play the percentages. In doing so you'll find yourself a great deal more successful than if you go for the outrageous shots that even the most elite players don't try. Therefore, always bear in mind that you should hit the shots you own and not the ones you don't own.

WATCH OUT FOR IDIOSYNCRACIES

When you're analyzing the game style of a pro, be sure to decide what the real performance attributes are and what causes the action to occur. A player can learn a great deal from examining how a professional athlete executes a certain stroke or movement pattern (see Figure 10-4), but you must look specifically at the total action, body part by body part.

Figure 10-3 In this photograph Vitas Gerulaitus is showing the crowd that he knows he made a mistake that he should not have made.

Figure 10-4 Instead of looking at the idiosyncrasies of a player like John McEnroe, be aware of the specific performance attributes that make him such a great player. Notice here on this return of serve that he has properly performed a unit turn and that his hips and shoulders are turned so he will optimize his angular momentum as he hits the return.

WHAT GOES INTO THE PERFECT STROKE?

Remember that to hit an effective stroke, good footwork is required not only to move but to generate a ground-reaction force (see Figure 10-5).

(a)   (b)

Figure 10-5(a), (b) Roscoe Tanner is said to have one of the best serves in the game of tennis. Notice here how he has not left the ground in this portion of his serve. Therefore, he generates a huge ground-reaction force and transfers that force effectively through his legs, hips, shoulders, and upper limb.

The force is then transferred through the hips and trunk to the upper limb, generating impetus for the racquet. Be aware that there is only one point in the entire motion when a stroke must be perfect: impact.

It really doesn't matter how you look during the backswing or during the follow-through, but only how the racquet hits the ball during the .004 second of impact. Some general statements hold true here. Although basic, they may help you.

1. If the ball goes too far upward off the racquet face, the racquet face is too open at impact;

2. If the ball travels into the net, the racquet face is too closed at impact;

3. If the ball goes to the right (for a right-handed player), the racquet head was angled in that direction;

4. If the ball travels to the left (for a right-handed player), the racquet head was angled in that direction; and

5. For the most effective impact, the racquet face should be nearly vertical.

USE OF A TEACHING PRO AND VISUAL AIDS

Due to the velocities and time durations of some of the situations I've just mentioned, it's virtually impossible for you to determine where a problem might lie in your stroke production. That's where trained professional teachers/coaches can help you (see Figure 10-6a). They have learned how each body part interacts with one another and the contribution of each to the total performance. However, there are times when even a trained eye has difficulty in detecting a movement error. This is where various types of visual aids can be extremely helpful (see Figure 10-6b). Still pictures, film, and videotape can all be of assistance to you and your instructor in analyzing how effective and efficient you are. This is because the high-speed action of a tennis stroke can be slowed so that each body part can be specifically examined.

Only one problem exists with this approach: Some athletes are so intrigued by seeing themselves in slow-motion and being able to effectively study their own games that they begin analyzing their strokes all the time. Sometimes this goes so far that they scrutinize their movements during match play, which can be seriously detrimental to performance. This phenomenon is called *paralysis by analysis*. Therefore, use a coach and visual aids as you need them but be careful not to get so involved with the analysis that it affects how you play. In that way you will reach your potential in tournament competition in the most efficient manner.

(a)   (b)

Figure 10-6(a), (b) In these pictures the author is seen working with touring pros Tom Gullikson (a) and his twin brother Tim Gullikson (b). In picture b you can see some of the photographic equipment the author uses to assist in analyzing the stroke production of the players he works with.

USE AN EFFECTIVE VELOCITY-ACCURACY TRADE-OFF

As you improve your skills and become involved in more high-level competition, you must be able to interchange velocity and accuracy at will. There will be times when it will be desirable to hit a high-velocity shot but the game of tennis is mostly a game of control. Seldom will it be necessary to hit the ball as hard as you can. A well-placed shot with medium speed is often much more important than a high-velocity, poorly placed stroke. More realistically, you need to vary velocities and ball spins to maintain optimal control and to prevent your opponent from becoming grooved to your strokes. As far as control goes, a few general playing tips may be helpful:

1. Be aware that if you must hit a ball from a corner of your court, a crosscourt shot allows you more court to hit toward (Figure 10-7);

2. When you hit a crosscourt shot, the ball will be traveling over the lowest part of the net (3-ft high in the middle vs. 3-ft 6-in high at the sidelines); and

3. Your most effective strokes will usually be deep in the opponent's court.

All of this, however, is dependent on how well you react to the emergency created by your opponent's previous shot.

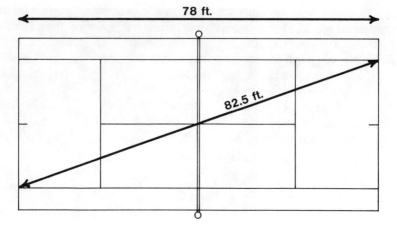

Figure 10-7 When you hit a ground stroke cross court, you have more court available to hit into, and the net is lower at the middle than at the sideline.

WORK ON ADAPTING TO EMERGENCIES

Just as you will try to dominate your opponent by varying your stroke production and placement, your opponent will be trying to do the same thing to you. That's why it's important that you not only develop effective footwork and strokes but also that you work on hitting effective returns of shots hit the same way (see Figure 10-8). That is, you must

(a)   **(b)**

Figure 10-8(a), (b) Here you can see John McEnroe caught in two different types of emergencies. Since he is such a great player, he has learned to adapt to various emergencies as they present themselves. Regardless of the situation he is presented with, we all know that he has the capability to create an even greater emergency for the opponent.

practice returning low-bouncing balls, high-bouncing balls, wide shots, deep shots, short shots, and balls with different spins on both sides— forehand and backhand. It will be necessary that you practice a serve-and-volley strategy and how to effectively hit an approach shot on a short ball. Once you get to the net, you must refine your low volley, high volley, touch volley, angled volley, and overhead smash. The list could continue but you are probably aware of the areas on which you must work. Whatever your priorities are in practicing to achieve a well-rounded tennis game, you must remember that everything occurring on the court during a match will be situational. Where the opponent is in his/her court, where you are in your court, and the shot your opponent has hit are some of the factors that will determine what shot you hit in return. And the only way to develop these areas is to practice them in a competitive setting like a practice match.

PRACTICING EFFECTIVELY

Practice doesn't make perfect. Perfect practice makes perfect. This expression seems to apply very appropriately to tennis. I've seen many players practice several hours a day for years and still not achieve the level they might have attained if they had practiced more effectively. This type of practice not only involves working with a good coach and being aware of your own stroke production, but also involves your mental attitude during practice sessions.

Many athletes don't learn from their mistakes. It's almost as though they keep practicing the same errors over and over. I suggest that as you practice you bear a few thoughts in mind:

1. Try not to make the same mistake twice (i.e., don't continually hit balls long, but use various forms of topspin combined with a slower velocity to gain confidence in the stroke and to regain your timing);
2. Have a determined attitude when you practice just as though you were in a match situation; and
3. Practice on all surfaces (hard court, clay, and grass) and in all situations (wind, bright sun, indoors, outdoors, and so on) so that you can accommodate your game whenever necessary.

ANTICIPATING ALL THE POSSIBILITIES

Anticipation in tennis deals with many facets of the game. One that I've already mentioned in this chapter is the emergency. As you play competitively, you will continually be placed in one emergency after another. Obviously, you must learn how to handle each predicament as it presents itself, and the only way to do this is to experience each one during match play. Practice sets and matches will help, but a player needs to become involved in sanctioned United States Tennis Association tournaments. Playing under the pressures of these tournaments is the only way you will become match tough. To get a schedule of tennis tournaments held at the national, sectional, or district (regional) level, request the information from the United States Tennis Association, 51 East 42nd Street, New York, NY 10017.

The second part of the game that requires some type of anticipation is understanding what the opponent is capable of doing during a point. You can use the sport science information presented in this book to actually analyze the opponent's game. This can be done during the warm-up and during the first few points of the match. As you warm up, for example, does the opponent hit deep and with heavy spin? If not, perhaps you will be able to attack by approaching the net on a short ball. When the warm-up is over, you should be able to generalize the opponent's capabilities. When the match begins you'll find out how correct you are. Your primary responsibility is to play your own game, but test the opponent when the situation arises. For instance, go to the net and see what happens. Don't be discouraged if you lose a point; the opponent may have hit a lucky shot. However, if you try something as a test of the opponent's capabilities in a certain situation and you lose several points doing it, you will need to change your strategy a bit. One possible change in strategy for the example I've mentioned might be for you to stay at your baseline and bring the opponent to the net. By now you may be aware of how important it is to be flexible with your strategy during a match. Sticking to one specific game plan could be your downfall.

The final type of anticipation necessary in competition is that of knowing your opponent's shot capabilities during a point as he/she is located on various parts of the court. For example, when McEnroe hits a very soft looping forehand that barely clears the net and dips toward his opponent who is located at the net, he will often take off running toward the net at the angle where he thinks the opponent will hit the ball. The television announcers will say that McEnroe's anticipatory capabilities are phenomenal. However, consider what options the opponent has available to him when McEnroe hits a short topspin shot that barely clears the net. The only shot the opponent can hit is a short angled drop shot. Therefore, McEnroe anticipates how and where the opponent will hit the ball before his own shot even clears the net and starts running for that position on the court. In actuality, instead of anticipating what the opponent will do, McEnroe sets himself up by forcing the opponent to hit a certain shot. You can also do this, but you must be able to answer such questions as:

- Can the opponent hit down the line on a wide shot?
- Does the opponent have good touch at the net?
- Does the opponent have a good overhead?
- How effective will that second serve be against me?
- When I go to the net, will the opponent attempt to pass me on one particular side each time?
- Can the opponent lob well?

These are but a few of the things true championship players are aware of when a match is in its early stages. Obviously, they don't have to ask themselves each question during a match. Through years of tournament competition, they have learned to recognize when the opponent has trouble performing a certain stroke under specific conditions. You can learn to have the same ability, but it may come to you quicker since you can employ your sport science background in making you a true championship player.

Index